REVOLUTIONARY LOVE
for Early Childhood Classrooms

Nurturing the Brilliance of Young Black Children

Gloria Swindler Boutte • Kamania Wynter-Hoyte
Nathaniel Bryan

Senior Vice President and Publisher: Tara Welty
Editorial Director: Sarah Longhi
Development Editors: Raymond Coutu & Tonya Leslie
Senior Editor: Shelley Griffin
Production Editor: Danny Miller
Creative Director: Tannaz Fassihi
Interior Designer: Maria Lilja

CONTENTS

This book is dedicated to the enduring influence of our esteemed scholar ancestors: Dr. Asa Hilliard, Dr. Frances Cress Welsing, Dr. Amos Wilson, and Dr. Janice Hale. Their profound scholarship, which celebrates the brilliance of Black children's culture, continues to inspire and guide us. With gratitude and a deep sense of responsibility, we carry their torch of knowledge, striving to create educational spaces where every Black child finds solace in the affirmation of their cultural identity and boundless potential in their brilliance.

ACKNOWLEDGMENTS

Gloria:

I honor and draw from decades of research by Black early childhood scholars like Drs. Asa Hilliard, Janice Hale, and Amos Wilson who made it clear that a child's racial identity is a key part of Black children's development. My scholarship, teaching, and service germinate from theirs. I thank my mentor, Nana (Queen) Dr. Joyce E. King, for all the insights that she so gracefully shares with me. I especially thank all the wonderful early childhood teachers and teacher educators who have heeded the call to be revolutionary in their teaching of Black children. Thank you.

Kamania:

I am deeply grateful for the teachers featured in this book and their revolutionary love of Black children. They pour into students every single day, even when their cups are empty.

I honor my late husband, Tiria Masinko Hoyte, who has loved me for nearly half of my life. I thank you for always supporting my aspirations and the work that I do as a teacher educator. I love you, today, tomorrow, and forever.

Nathaniel:

I would like to acknowledge my mother and first teacher, Barbara Bryan, who is the epitome of revolutionary love, and my entire family whose tireless effort and commitment have sustained me throughout my life! Thank you for showing me how to love in revolutionary ways.

FOREWORD

by Tonia R. Durden

Recently I had the honor and blessing to attend Beyoncé's Renaissance World Tour and experience her Black excellence and revolutionary love for Black music, culture, and our way of grooving in spaces that are often hostile, violent, and oppressive. Wearing my girlfriend-vetted wig, black sliver sequin top, cut-off shorts, and sparkly cowgirl boots (check out that imagery!), I leaned into the joy, brilliance, and power of Blackness, as I sang along, grooved, and danced. It was an experience that continues to sustain me and remind me of what African scholar Asa Hilliard calls the *maroon within us*—the collective development of Black people, including our charge to value it, honor it, call upon it, be proud of it, and defend it.

My name is Tonia Durden, mother of Zoe, daughter of Cora, granddaughter of Bertha, and great-granddaughter of Addie (Who run the world? Girls!). As the self-proclaimed Beyoncé of Academia, I am a "survivor" of the segregated, integrated, segregated southern early learning and school system. In my work as a teacher educator and researcher, I unapologetically and enthusiastically "slay" and "ring the alarm" on practices and experiences that do not cultivate the cultural and academic excellence of Black children.

I eagerly turn up the volume on educators, scholars, and leaders who reimagine education for Black children and are committed to promoting Black excellence and brilliance. I promote the "Black Parade" of scholarship, resources, and books that focus on the ways Black children, families, teachers, and communities can thrive and demonstrate our ancestral excellence. With that in mind, I humbly ask—Are you ready to experience a revolutionary love experience all about championing Black children?

With this book, authors Gloria Swindler Boutte, Kamania Wynter-Hoyte, and Nathaniel Bryan take readers through a multidimensional, multi-rhythmic experience of having and practicing revolutionary love for Black children. This is not a sit-in-your-seat-and-read-page-by-page book. Instead, it's the kind of book that will make you want to sing, clap, and shout *"Right on!"* Be ready to experience how the authors emphasize the importance of the centering Black voices, experiences, brilliance, and literacies and model them throughout the text.

In the first few chapters, the authors discuss the importance of disrupting the various forms of anti-Black violence that occur in classrooms and instead honor Black culture through harmony, expression, and communication. With just the right tempo and bass, they feature remarkable teachers, such as Mr. Benson, Ms. Collins, and Ms. Baines, as guides to revolutionary loving instruction.

From there, the authors shine a spotlight on Neka, Ms. Makey, Megan, Kwame, Ms. Smith, Ms. Collins, and Ms. Gaither, who create joyful play spaces for children and honor daily the beauty and power of African American languages and literacies. As the finale, the authors take you into the deep groove of revolutionary loving instruction by introducing the African Diaspora Literacy framework and curriculum that reflects and honors Black people's culture, ancestral roots, and herstories and histories.

This is a Black-centric book. In every chapter, you'll find opportunities to pause and reflect on the knowledge shared, consider what you can do in the upcoming days and weeks, and think about how you can extend what you're learning beyond the classroom.

Not only will you receive the foundational knowledge needed to proceed with revolutionary love for Black children by implementing the authors' Believe, Know, and Do framework, you will also discover wonderful children's books and songs as well as teaching strategies you can begin using immediately.

Beyoncé's concert lifted my spirits. Her Black excellence recharged my Black excellence. This book had a similar effect on me. Each voice, experience, resource, and scholarly contribution served to anchor to my own work in cultivating the cultural and academic excellence of Black children. I have no doubt that you, too, will experience the same revolutionary love experience while reading this book. Lean into its rhythms and don't hesitate to replay parts of it. Sing along, teach along, read along, dance along, and be inspired to *be lovin' Black children* and *be teachin'* in a revolutionary loving way. I hope you enjoy, as I did, this latest greatest hit by Gloria, Kamania, and Nathaniel.

Tonia R. Durden
Clinical Professor & Birth-Five Program Coordinator
Georgia State University Department of
Early Childhood & Elementary Education

INTRODUCTION

We love you! How does it feel to hear those words? You may wonder, because we don't even know you, how could we love you? But have you ever expressed love for someone you don't know? For example, have you ever expressed love for a baby that is about to be born into your family? A baby you've yet to meet, but you know you love? Likewise, many of us love entertainers, athletes, actors, politicians, and other celebrities whom we have never met and probably will never meet. Ours include Beyoncé, John Legend, Michelle Obama, Michael Jordan, and Idris Elba.

We say *I love you* because we appreciate and respect the foundational role that you play, as an early childhood educator, in the lives of young children. Think of our proclamation of love for you as *revolutionary love*.

We honor the poet Kalamu ya Salaam (1978), who first coined the term "revolutionary love." He writes:

> We are lovers
> and revolutionaries
> conscious that our commitment to each other
> serves higher purpose
> than limited personal pleasure

Revolutionary love transcends mushy or surface-level love. It is deep love designed to liberate all children. In this book, we position revolutionary love as an antidote to interrupt anti-Blackness faced by Black children *and* their teachers. It is reenergizing love that reminds us of the purpose for which we entered the field—the betterment of children. Matias and Allen (2013) explain, "Love is a state of existence, a way of being in the world, that leads us back together. It is a feeling that is paid forward in the interconnectedness of our humanity and its capacity to produce conditions that are more just."

At a time when teachers are being vilified for so many reasons, we proudly assert that you are amazing! With this book, we aim to inspire a renaissance of respect for and among teachers. Revolutionary love is the love of humanity and the acknowledgment that all children have the *human right* to be taught in ways that makes sense to them culturally. We aim to help you see and honor the humanity, intelligence, ethnic and racial identities, and linguistic practices of your students and use those assets to build curriculum for and with your students. Revolutionary love nurtures all students by disrupting messages of racial inferiority, exclusion and omission, and historical misrepresentations in early childhood spaces.

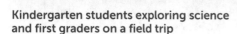

Kindergarten students exploring science and first graders on a field trip

Who Are We?

This work is near and dear to our hearts. We are three teacher educators with decades of experience in teaching and scholarship. In this section, we introduce each author and our journey in writing this book rooted in revolutionary love. As you read our stories, we invite you to recognize the important role you play as protectors of Black children. Our collective wish is that Black children everywhere will be immersed in revolutionary early childhood classrooms and instructional practices that honor their whole selves.

Gloria

As far back as I can remember, I have been concerned about the welfare of young children—starting as a big sister and then as a teen babysitter. Majoring in early childhood education as an undergraduate and in child development as a graduate student just made sense and fit me like a glove. Having my own children, and now grandchildren, certainly elevated my concern. As the elder among the three authors, with adult children and grandchildren, I bring intergenerational insights about and experiences with Black children—personally and professionally.

I am currently a Professor and Associate Dean, dedicated to spreading revolutionary love. But in my earlier roles as preschool teacher, child development specialist, and college instructor specializing in child development and early childhood education, I whitewashed the advice and guidance I offered professionals, parents, and preservice and in-service teachers. I was well-versed in the ideas of theorists such as Piaget, Vygotsky, and Bronfenbrenner, as well as developmental norms, and advised and guided those stakeholders accordingly. I read and wrote for *Young Children, Dimensions in Education*, and other ECE journals.

While I was always interested in the welfare of Black children, I was far from *revolutionary*. For example, in one well-funded, four-year study of 100 African American children and their families, I focused on the importance of parents engaging their preschoolers in reading. Retrospectively, I do not recall *any* of the books the research team and I recommended focusing on Black families and children. For the duration of the study, we dutifully presented and taught parents to use prefabricated lessons and never once asked them for ideas or recognized the many ways they used their literacies at home and in community, every day. Those realizations did not come to me until the end of the study and the final data analysis. I had been too caught up thinking about having a "well-designed study," using narrow, Eurocentric research methods, to go deeper and humanize the investigation.

Hopefully, this book makes up for missed opportunities on my part by highlighting the damage done to Black children in ECE settings—and what you, as caring educators, can do about it.

In my current work as a teacher educator, I provide support to ECE teachers on their journeys to embracing revolutionary love. I know firsthand how what we teach may not align with our love of Black children. In professional development with teachers and in undergraduate and graduate courses, I begin by asking my students to reflect on what they believe about Black children beyond superficial comments such as "I love all children." My students and I spend time reflecting on home, school, books and other media, and evoking memories, to do deep archeological dives (nod to Yolanda Sealey-Ruiz) into what we believe and how we came to believe it. We spend time discussing how anti-Blackness is endemic in ECE settings and society, and come to understand that any of us can contribute to it. We examine classroom book collections, resources, and lessons. I introduce them to knowledge bases that I know have the power to transform. And I do all of this without judgment and with deep appreciation for teachers. My students begin by trying out one or two ideas in the classroom—say reading a book or playing a song. As they get positive reactions from children and families, they typically continue on the trajectory toward revolutionary loving instruction, which you will learn about in this book.

I practice and promote revolutionary love at home, as well as at work. I am a mother of two children, one boy and one girl. With both children, I was a highly involved and zealous mom. For example, right before my second child, Jonathan, was born, the U.S. Consumer Product Safety Commission issued a recall on vinyl mini-blinds made before July 1996. Concern was expressed that vinyl in some mini-blinds could deteriorate from sunlight and heat and cause lead dust to form, thus presenting a lead-poisoning hazard to young children. With the quickness of a supermom, I immediately replaced all 25 vinyl mini-blinds in our home with aluminum blinds. Of paramount concern was the safety of my Jonathan, the new baby we were expecting. We understood that our duty as parents was to keep him safe.

For both children, I tried my best to ensure that they would be well in this world. Even before they were born, I:

- ate healthy foods, visited the doctor regularly, and took prenatal vitamins
- prepared a beautiful, stimulating space for babies and safety-proofed the home
- read to the babies while carrying them

After they were born, we continued to ensure their wellness by:

- facilitating their cognitive, social, racial, physical, emotional, and cultural development
- engaging with family and spending quality time with them each day
- teaching them about their history and culture
- exposing them to the global world via texts, experiences, and travel
- laughing, dancing, and talking with them
- preparing them for school

We sent our children to school with a prayer that educators would see them how we did. Despite our best intentions, planning, and hopes for them, we soon realized that our ability to protect them in schools and society is limited at best. To be clear, neither child encountered educators who were malicious or mean. Yet, our children were bombarded with Eurocentric curriculum and countless microaggressions. For example, Jonathan was overlooked for placement on the academic team although he had top scores on all standardized tests and straight As. Stephanie's second grade teacher gave her a "B" because (as the teacher boldly told us) "she was not an 'A' student" even though the points for all assignments fell into the 'A' range (Boutte, 1992). In both cases, my husband and I were able to remedy the situation, but the damage was already done and was not unnoticed by my children. I can name dozens of other personal examples (as well as those cited in professional literature and stories of friends). None of these are isolated cases. Cumulatively, these are attacks on Black humanity.

I am happy to share that when my husband and I made our children's teachers aware of any concerns, most teachers were eager to remedy the situation—since we all had the goal of ensuring that *the children were well*. I invite you to think with me about ways that Black children like mine are not being protected and elevated in classrooms.

Regardless of the configuration of schools (e.g., rural, suburban, urban, racially segregated, or integrated), Black children continue to be assaulted by curricular invisibility, distortions, irrelevance, and inaccuracies (Boutte & Bryan, 2021; Love, 2016). For example, recently, school districts across the country have tried to ban a book that tells the real-life story of Ruby Bridges, who, as a child, paved the way to integrating schools in Louisiana. The offense? The idea that the book might make some White children feel bad.

In spite of our efforts to ensure that they are well emotionally, socially, psychologically, physically, and cognitively, our children receive the message that being Black carries with it a deeply rooted stigma—though many Black children and families do not readily recognize that or are able to name it as such. That said, there are also many Black families trying to find positive counternarratives to share with their children. And while we do our best, it is not enough to protect our children in educational settings, though these same schools serve as a refuge for White children.

Kamania

As a young child, I would always play school with my dolls. I would line them up and teach them reading, writing, and arithmetic. Years later, as a high school student, it came as no surprise to my parents when I told them I wanted to be an early childhood educator.

I spent my first 14 years of life in Brooklyn, New York, and my adolescent years in South Florida. So I was constantly surrounded by diverse communities. I learned so much about other cultures, languages, and ways of being from my friends and their families. But I didn't learn much about Black histories (pre-slavery), Black languages, and Black culture in school. I distinctly remember my elementary teachers Mrs. Griffith, Mrs. Kaufman, and Mrs. Cohen because they taught me about Black excellence.

My first job was teaching kindergarten in a school outside of Atlanta, Georgia, that served primarily African American, Latine, and Vietnamese families. So it was important to take a multicultural approach. Now, as a teacher educator and researcher, I realize the many areas where I fell short. As much as I loved my students, I was not teaching and testing them in revolutionary ways. I was teaching them in Eurocentric ways.

Through my graduate work, I became acquainted with the work of Black scholars such as Asa Hilliard, Joyce E. King, Catheri Dorsey-Gaines, and

Geneva Smitherman. From them, I learned about African American Language (AAL) and that it is rule-governed, one of the rules being the omission of certain ending sounds. My mind went immediately to my kindergarten student whose responses I incorrectly marked as wrong when she was simply speaking her first language.

Fast forward to the summer of 2018, when I became a mother for the first time. In addition to the joys of motherhood, I experienced so many emotions, such as appreciation for access to health care, anxiety over the high mortality rate of Black mothers, exhaustion from sleepless nights, and frustration that my husband did not receive paternity leave. During my sleepless nights, my mind wandered. I thought about my ancestors, who were denied the right to see their own children grow up. They never got to see the kinds of people their children grew up to be. That same summer, Latine children were being separated from their families at the U.S. border. All these thoughts consumed me, as I rocked my son to sleep and kissed his forehead. When Langston was three months old, I finally felt comfortable to take him out in public. At restaurants, people often stopped us to say how adorable he was. I smiled like a proud mother and said thank you.

But deep down inside, I know there will come a time when he is not seen as adorable, and I will have to have some difficult discussions with him in order for him to come home to me, unlike Tamir Rice who didn't go home to his mother because he was murdered at the age of 12 for playing.

I am now a mother of two young children, and when I teach preservice and in-service teachers, I ask myself, "Would I trust these teachers with my children?" "Am I confident they will love my children's languages, cultures, self-expression, and play, critically and authentically?"

How do I know that my children's essence is cultivated and not *spiritually murdered* (Love, 2016)? And this is not limited to the adults in the building, but I often wonder what teachers are doing to educate all children, no matter how those children identify racially or ethnically, and if they are aware of the beauty and excellence of Black people. Specifically, are they teaching through a pro-Black (Boutte et. al, 2021; Boutte & Compton-Lilly, 2022) and humanizing lens? If so, how? According to Derman-Sparks (2011), if that kind of teaching isn't happening, Black students are not the only ones to suffer. White students will learn inaccurate, incomplete, and distorted information and, in turn, absorb messages of White superiority and whiteness as the norm. Therefore, I do this work not to simply ensure that my children, Langston and Nyla, are well, but to try to make sure that all children are.

Nathaniel

I started my professional teaching career in an urban high school in Columbia, South Carolina. I noticed immediately the institutional and structural inequities (e.g., limited resources, unqualified teachers, etc.) the predominantly Black student population faced. Three years later, I transitioned to an early childhood/elementary school—

teaching French to third to fifth graders. I noticed the persistence of similar inequities I had witnessed at the high school level. Revolutionary love was nonexistent in this school! I wanted to see that change. To that end, I worked with colleagues to cultivate a revolutionary loving school environment by providing professional development on culturally relevant/responsive teachings to my colleagues who were eager to learn strategies to better support the academic and social needs of students. I also created mentoring clubs to support Black boys who rarely felt revolutionary love from the school's faculty and staff. They were often misunderstood, and such misunderstanding often led to suspension and expulsion from school. These boys reminded me of my nephew Jerrell who was a newborn at that time. At that moment, my work became both personal and professional. As an early career teacher, I knew I needed to work with teachers to change the conditions of early childhood education so that Jerrell and the Black boys I taught could feel both the warmth and revolutionary love of the school community.

The desire to change the conditions of early childhood education to better support Black boys led to my pursuit of a professional career in school administration, and later academia. Both careers prompted me to turn up the volume in my racial justice work. This work is most pronounced in academia where I prepare teachers to teach all children, but especially Black children who long for revolutionary loving teachers. When we early childhood educators focus on racial justice work and begin to see all Black children as our own, we can change the conditions in which they are schooled. That change begins by centering revolutionary love in our teaching of every Black child, in every classroom. I believe we owe it to them to repair what is and has been broken in our school system. That repair begins by repaying our longstanding educational debt (the neglect of pedagogical, curricular, financial resources that ensure Black children are well in our schools; Ladson-Billings, 2009) by committing to revolutionary love in our early childhood classrooms. I look forward to taking this journey with you.

Collectively, the three of us have taught thousands of in-service and preservice teachers and administrators to honor Black children in their early childhood classrooms, and they are grateful for the insights they gain. After completing a course entitled Educating African American Students, one very seasoned ECE administrator (Saudah Collins) concluded, "I have to go back in the classroom now that I know how to teach Black students. I wish I had this information when I went through my teacher education program." True to her word, she resigned from administration and began teaching first grade. More than a decade later, she is still teaching. She offers an African studies course at an elementary school, for children in K–5. Some of her work is featured in this book.

In this book, you will get a chance to meet Ms. Collins and share her joy of teaching Black students and about Black perspectives that are often ignored. Her sentiments about being excited about teaching Black children are not uncommon. You will meet other ECE teachers with whom we have worked or are currently working. They are women and men from a range of ethnic groups. They recognize that their teacher preparation programs did not prepare them to teach Black students effectively. They missed out on content, strategies, frameworks, and examples like the ones shared in this book. But they are committed to being powers *for good for all children*.

Why This Book

As an early childhood educator, you contribute to children's cognitive, academic, social, emotional, physical, and cultural well-being. By providing classroom examples and activities that you can do right away, we hope to help you with that major responsibility to make a positive impact on the lives of Black children and their peers who are watching what's happening in the world and learning from it.

This book builds on *Revolutionary Love: Creating a Culturally Inclusive Literacy Classroom* (Wynter-Hoyte et al., 2022), which describes what revolutionary love looks like in elementary classrooms. A primary goal of this book is to activate and energize early childhood educators so they will view teaching young African American students as exhilarating and rewarding rather than as problematic and laborious. We aim to facilitate critical transformations of early childhood educators and classrooms.

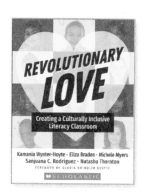

Framework for This Book

In each chapter we use a three-part framework that we first discussed in *Revolutionary Love: Creating a Culturally Inclusive Classroom* (Wynter-Hoyte et al., 2022):

1. Believe
2. Know
3. Do

We provide strategies that you can reflect on, begin to understand, and use in your respective early childhood education spaces.

Three-Part Framework: Believe, Know, Do

Believe	Know	Do
Teachers who embrace revolutionary love understand that what they believe is foundational to the ways they engage with students. They are committed to examining and disrupting any beliefs that are deficit-oriented so that their practices are affirming of the students they teach.	**Teachers who embrace revolutionary love understand the importance of knowing their students, and the resources they use to teach them.** They are knowledgeable about their students' cultural and linguistic identities and the systems that marginalize their students, as well as the practices they can use to affirm the students they teach.	**Teachers who embrace revolutionary love understand that what they do—their practice—needs to be loving, liberatory, and affirming.** They center their students' identities and cultural heritage and intentionally create learning communities for and with students so that students feel seen, heard, and valued.

Used with permission: Wynter-Hoyte, K., Braden, E., Myers, M., Rodriguez, S. C., & Thornton, N. (2022).

n because they love children. As
ents such as, *I love all my students
hether they are Black, White,*
rs *do not see color*, they do not
ization, and resilience of Black
olutionary loving instruction is not
dren's humanity.

lt times and in the face of harsh
y Love: Creating a Culturally
yte et al., 2022), Gloria states, "As
love ain't. Thin love ain't love at
eived in school was thin indeed.
l transformational" (p. 10). Enjoy a
like in classrooms.

at is your
?

**PAUSE &
REFLECT**

Chapter 1

ESTABLISHING A REVOLUTIONARY LOVE MINDSET AND PRACTICE

SECOND-GRADE TEACHER JANICE BAINES IS A revolutionary loving teacher. One of the first things children hear when they enter her classroom are songs such as "These Three Words" by Stevie Wonder. While serenading them, she conveys that she loves them unconditionally, just the way they are. She lets them know that they are always enough. Teachers can create their own songs using similar lyrics like the ones below that were created after listening to Stevie Wonder's song. These can be sung to the melody in the song. Some words can be parts of speech *and* high- frequency words (e.g., little, good). Basking in this loving welcome, children relax and lean into their authentic selves. Ms. Baines layers the message of love in her instruction, using lyrics from "These Three Words" to engage children in shared reading and to teach high-frequency words, adjectives, nouns, and number words. She also makes her love for her students clear by introducing an Adinkra symbol, Akoma, from the Akan people in West Africa, which represents the values of patience, goodwill, faithfulness, endurance, and tolerance. Children in Janice Baines' classroom come to understand that Black culture is deep and rich.

Akoma (Adinkra symbol)

> **Ms. Baines's Assignment for "Three Little Words"**
>
> **YELLOW:** High-frequency words
>
> **BLUE:** Adjectives
>
> **GREEN:** Nouns
>
> **RED:** Number words
>
> [CHORUS]
>
> Three little words
>
> Not very hard
>
> Three little words
>
> Easy and sweet
>
> Three little words
>
> Forever loving
>
> Makes our heart
>
> Feel good inside.

What Do Revolutionary Loving Teachers BELIEVE?

Revolutionary loving teachers like Ms. Baines routinely integrate music and other literacies into their practice. They find out the music children hear at home and then come up with creative ways to teach curriculum goals and standards based on that music and other texts (e.g., movie clips, videos).

What Do You *Believe* About Black Children?

An important first step on your journey to revolutionary loving teaching is to reflect on what you believe about Black children. So take a moment to do that.

> **PAUSE & REFLECT**
>
> ▶ **Write down as many stereotypes that you know about Black children (socially, culturally, emotionally, cognitively, physically).** They can be positive or negative. You do not have to believe that they are true, but write them down anyway.
>
> ▶ **Write down as many stereotypes that you know about Black families.** Again, you do not need to believe them.
>
> ▶ **Write down as many strengths as you can think of about Black children and families.**
>
> ▶ **Do you believe that the same curriculum and instructional practices that work for White children also work for Black children?**
>
> These reflections will help you become aware of what societal beliefs exist for Black children. This is an important first step and will relate to how these covert and overt beliefs get translated into ECE curriculum and instruction that we will discuss later. Interestingly, when we do these reflection activities with educators, many teachers struggle to come up with strengths that Black children have. Often, the strengths that they do come up with are related to physical prowess. Many cultural strengths

such as linguistic dexterity, emotional intelligence, and cognitive savviness are not mentioned. If these were not included on your list of strengths, no worries. We have all been influenced by societal beliefs in ways that escape our notice. This book will help you refocus and reframe negative stereotypes about Black people which lead to overlooking the holistic strengths of Black children. If these strengths were on your list, you will find these beliefs about Black children to be foundational for revolutionary teaching.

What Do Revolutionary Loving Teachers KNOW?

Revolutionary loving teachers like Ms. Baines recognize the long-standing body of knowledge that explains how Black children's strengths and needs are overlooked daily in ECE settings (Boutte & Bryan, 2021; Hale & Hale, 1982; Love, 2016). Ms. Baines is intentional about ensuring that Black children in her classroom feel loved. Elsewhere, we have explained five types of blind spots in everyday school practices that Black children encounter: 1) physical; 2) symbolic, 3) linguistic, 4) curricular/pedagogical, and 5) systemic. Because these actions, and inactions in some cases, are harmful and traumatic to Black children, we define them as types of violence against Black children's culture and humanity though they often escape the notice of ECE educators. If we are to create revolutionary loving classrooms for Black children, we have to begin with an understanding of the current state of affairs. These five types of violence are referred to as anti-Black violence because they disrespect and attack Black humanity.

Five Types of Anti-Black Violence

1. **Physical violence** refers to bodily assault on Black children such as hitting, pushing, and beating. For example, as reported in *The New York Times*, a six-year-old Black girl in Orlando, Florida, was arrested and handcuffed for having a temper tantrum at school (Zaveri, 2020). Physical violence also refers to the residual health effects (e.g., high blood pressure, anxiety) of enduring ongoing anti-Black aggressions and discrimination.

2. **Symbolic violence** includes racial abuse against the spirit and humanity of Black children. It is played out in educational settings when educators misread Black children's culture, silence their voices, and reject their experiences and lived realities. Common examples include making disparaging remarks about Black children's names, hairstyles, and cultural ways of dressing. Sometimes, the symbolic violence can be seen in physical and academic harm toward children. For instance, a Milwaukee teacher cut the hair of a Black first grader because she was playing with her beads. Research shows that the highest suspension rates for Black children are in preschool (Gilliam et al., 2016).

3. **Linguistic violence** entails the marginalizing and policing of African American Language (AAL). Likewise, characterizing AAL as "broken English," "incorrect," or "not good" is linguistically violent. Privileging Standard English and devaluing connections between language, race, and identity are also examples.

4. **Curricular and pedagogical (instructional) violence** occurs when the curriculum is irrelevant, inaccurate, distorted, and incomplete. Sanitized and/or deficit-based versions of Black history are taught. Pedagogical violence is committed when educators unintentionally and/or intentionally minimize how a teacher positionally shapes curricular decisions and instructional practices. In teacher education programs, Black literacy theories and Black-informed research are commonly absent, contributing

to anti-Black attitudes.

5. **Systemic school violence** is ingrained in educational structures, processes, discourses, customs, policies, and laws. A typical example is the use of invalid assessments to measure Black students' language and literacy. As early as preK, Black children are expelled in greater numbers than their non-Black peers for the same behavior (Okonofua et al., 2016).

What Do You *Know* About Black Children's Experiences In School?

An important part of your journey to revolutionary loving teaching is reflecting on your background knowledge about Black children's experiences in educational settings. Take a moment to pause and reflect on your knowledge base.

PAUSE & REFLECT

▶ Did you have any courses on Black children in your teacher preparation program or in your professional development as a teacher?

▶ What theories, research, books, and articles about Black children did you study in your teacher preparation program or professional development as a teacher?

▶ What research or information about Black children have you encountered since?

What Do Revolutionary Loving Teachers DO?

While physical violence is often easy to name and call out, the other four types of violence are more covert and often go unnoticed by ECE educators. Nonetheless, none of them is rare. Revolutionary educators assume that all humans deserve the right to dignity, equity, and freedom. Teachers who want to ensure that Black children are well watch for these types of violence and certainly do not contribute to them. They do not gloss over Black children's experiences. They take the foundational steps to recognize what they do *not* know and familiarize themselves with bodies of knowledge that recognize and celebrate Black children's experiences. Revolutionary love can eradicate all types of violence in ECE settings. It is a love that humanizes Black children and recognizes the interconnectedness of us all. Black children do not commit these types of violence on themselves, so it takes all of us to stop

those who do and fight for the liberation and betterment of Black children. Later in the chapter, we offer a few guiding points for doing just that. Throughout the book, we offer many specific examples and things you can do right now.

What Can You DO NOW in the Classroom?

1. **Acknowledge that anti-Black violence in society and schools is real.** This includes physical, symbolic, curriculum/instructional, linguistic and systemic violences.

2. **Take some time to reflect on how anti-Black violence exists in your center, school, and/or district.** Even if this makes you feel uncomfortable, be okay with experiencing discomfort on behalf of the children.

3. **Brainstorm one or two actionable steps to combat anti-Black violence in your center, school, and/or district.** For example, examine all of the classroom book collections to see if Black people and culture are positively and adequately represented. Here are some sample questions:

   - Are Black people included in this text? Why or why not?
   - Do you see anything unfair to Black people? Tell me more about this.
   - Who or what is shown as necessary to the story? How was the message of importance conveyed?
   - Are Black people left out or shown as unimportant? How was this message conveyed?
   - Can the message of this story be hurtful or unfair to Black people? Why?
   - How does the text make you feel? Why?
   - What can you do to improve your collection of children's literature? (Muller, 2021)

4. **Linguistically, look closely at an upcoming literacy lesson that you plan to teach.** Consider the following:

   - Are Black people represented in this lesson?
   - If so, is the information accurate?
   - As needed, make changes by adding a book, song, or other text that represents Black culture in a positive way.
   - Note how children react when you teach the updated lesson.

While supporting children as they practice writing, simultaneously affirm their racial identities. Children's lived experiences should be a part of your curriculum. For example, you may have children bring in examples of hair products that they use at home as a way to launch an activity about hair joy. Continue to weave racial identity affirmation into literacy throughout the day.

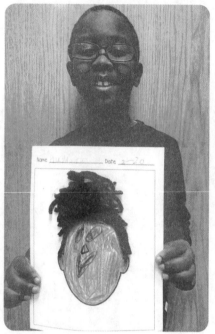

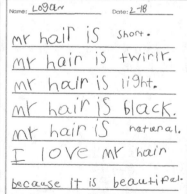

Name: Logan   Date: 2-18

mr hair is short.
mr hair is twirlr.
mr hair is light.
mr hair is black.
mr hair is natural.
I love mr hair
because it is beautiful.

Name: Jayce   Date: 2-21

I love my hair because
it is soft.
I love my hair because it is cool.
I love my hair because
it is manageable.
I love my hair because
it is curly.
I love my hair
because it makes me
feel important.

Black children explore their hair stories.

Revolutionary Love for Early Childhood Classrooms

What Can You DO IN THE UPCOMING WEEKS?

1. **Symbolically:** Include positive images of Black people and cultures on bulletin boards and wall displays, such as photographs of children's families and their communities, or you may display picture books such as *The Modern Day Black Alphabet*, which showcases the beauty of Black communities through stunning photography.

2. **Curricularly:** Look for omissions and inaccuracies, even when it is difficult to spot them. Whose cultures, communities, and experiences are centered in the curriculum? Take the necessary steps to center Black cultures, communities, and experiences in your lessons.

3. **Linguistically:** Welcome and build on any languages that children speak. By doing so, you help them maintain linguistic and cultural bonds with their families and communities. This includes African American Language (see discussion in Chapter 4). When you embrace the use of a child's African American Language, the child will leave school knowing *There is nothin' wrong wit da way she be talkin'*. This is revolutionary because it is not the message most speakers of African American Language hear in school.

After learning about Madame C. J. Walker, first-grade students created their own hair products during science centers.

What Can You DO BEYOND YOUR CLASSROOM?

1. **Discuss with your team, grade level, and/or school the five types of anti-Black violence.** Consider creating a PowerPoint presentation around types of violence using your own examples or some that we've shared to build awareness of how they show up in schools.

2. **Take a close look at your center or school's policies regarding restorative disciplinary practices.** Are Black children disproportionately affected by those policies? If so, what needs to change?

Ms. Smith and students at a state museum

What Revolutionary Loving Teachers Believe, Know, and Do

Examples of Anti-Black School Violence	Revolutionary Loving Teachers		
	Believe	**Know**	**Do**
Physical Black children across the nation (a five-year-old in Maryland, a six-year-old in Orlando, a seven-year-old in Flint) are handcuffed and placed in law enforcement cars for having a tantrum.	That physical violence is unacceptable, no matter its severity.	That ensuring physical well-being is necessary in order to foster critical consciousness, teacher-child relationships, and communalism.	• Acknowledge and interrupt racial profiling and physical handling of Black children. • Treat Black children's bodies with the same level of respect as those of White children.
Symbolic Black children are denied the right to be themselves in schools such as a six-year-old in Pensacola being expelled because of his locs and a Milwaukee teacher cutting off a first grader's beaded braids in class.	That symbolic violence devalues Black children's sense of identity.	That if teachers value Black culture, their expectations will match the great potential for success and individual expression that Black children have.	• Provide affirmations of Black people and culture in imagery (e.g., pictures, newsletters). Include voices and experiences of Black people throughout the year. • Validate the cultural hairstyles and dress styles of Black children.
Linguistic Black children are taught that African American Language (AAL) is "broken English" and "incorrect," and that code-switching is the best approach to "master" Standard English.	• That languages are tied to identities and Black children are bi/multilingual. • That AAL is a rule-governed and legitimate language.	That if teachers value Black language(s), AAL, or African American Vernacular English, they honor Black students' heritage, families, and communities.	• Value AAL by providing books that affirm it and engaging AAL speakers and other children in discussions about AAL. • Include opportunities for AAL to be used in speaking, writing, and reading activities.

Examples of Anti-Black School Violence	Revolutionary Loving Teachers		
	Believe	Know	Do
Curricular/Pedagogical First- through third-grade students are given instructional material that dehumanizes enslaved Africans (e.g., word math problems that reference slaves picking cotton and getting beatings, asking students to calculate the amount of cotton picked and/or the number of whippings) in California, Georgia, and New York.	Whether unintentional or intentional, teachers often make curricular decisions that harm Black children.	• Curriculum should be African-centered. • Curriculum should include perspectives of African American and other African Diasporic people.	• Provide ongoing, accurate, and comprehensive inclusion of heritages of people from the African diaspora (including African Americans). Provide accurate historical accounts. • Engage students in critical dialogue and critical literacy. • Begin the history of Black people with African history.
Systemic Black preschool students are suspended from school—such as Tunette Powell's two Black preschool sons being suspended a total of eight times in the same year—while White peers whose behaviors were similar or worse were given more appropriate admonishments or no punishments at all.	While this may be unintentional, traditional Eurocentric education policies and practices are often inherently anti-Black.	Inherently anti-Black policies and practices in early childhood practices will truncate the potential and possibilities of Black children.	Work to initiate and facilitate systemic changes in school policies (e.g., access to gifted programs; suspension/expulsion policies revised to allow for restorative discipline).

PAUSE & REFLECT

▶ Consider what school might feel like for Black children who experience various types of anti-Black violence daily.

▶ What messages do students who witness violence at school receive?

▶ Have you ever witnessed any of these types of violence at school? If so, what was your response?

As you move forward, the first step is to take a quick inventory of your classroom and school to evaluate current practices and to begin thinking about what you can do if changes are needed. As an informal activity, complete the form below. This is for your reflections only and does not have to be shared until you learn more about how to honor Black children in your classroom and school. What do you notice? How do you feel? How do you think Black children feel? Remember that your efforts for transformational teaching are done on behalf of the children.

Practices	Observations	Your Reflection
Physical	Are Black children being treated physically with respect and care by educators?	
Symbolic	In what ways are Black cultural expressions (e.g., names, hairstyles, dress) honored?	
Linguistic	Are educators knowledgeable about African American Language? Are Black students validated when they speak AAL?	
Instructional/ Curricular	Are there a variety of books and other texts (e.g., music, videos, web pages, curriculum) reflecting Black people in positive and substantive ways?	
Systemic	What school/classroom policies (e.g., assessments, home-school communications) support Pro-Black teaching? How can you and your colleagues implement them?	

Template available at scholastic.com/revlove-early-resources

Chapter 2

HONORING BLACK CULTURE IN THE CLASSROOM... EVERY DAY

ONE OF THE FAVORITE BOOKS AMONG THE FOUR-YEAR-olds in Mr. Benson's classroom is *I Am Enough* by Grace Byers. At the children's request, Mr. Benson reads it aloud several times each month, and during his readings, children engage in *movement*, acting out parts of the book, such as singing or flying. Mr. Benson loves that the book captures the *harmony* of nature and a range of *emotions* that humans experience. Though the children may not realize it, the book mirrors Black culture in many ways and captures cultural attributes such as movement, spirituality, expressive individualism, and communalism. *I Am Enough* reinforces the idea that children have a *purpose in life* and can become their best selves.

Mr. Benson routinely uses this book, along with other books, music, artwork, and videos, to validate and welcome Black children and ensures they know that they are enough just as they are.

To teach in revolutionary loving ways, ECE teachers need to recognize overt and covert ways that violence (physical, symbolic, linguistic, curricular/instructional, and systemic) appears in educational settings. In this way, you can interrupt and counter violence in your own setting. There are many ways to interrupt the five different types of violence in educational settings. In this chapter, we will demonstrate things you can do right now to honor Black cultural ways of being.

What Do Revolutionary Loving Teachers BELIEVE?

In revolutionary classrooms, ECE teachers believe in ensuring the cultural competence of African American children. To ensure Black children's cultural competence, teachers must help them: 1) learn about their own culture, and 2) learn about cultures other than their own (Ladson-Billings, 2009). Revolutionary loving teachers believe that children's cultural development should be honored in the classroom every day. They also understand that children need to learn about other children's cultures. Teachers recognize that many aspects of life in the classroom, including materials and interaction styles, are cultural reflections. For example, Mr. Benson can clearly see that *I Am Enough* is a cultural reflection for his students, who love the book because of how it resonates with their own lives.

Revolutionary love teachers Ms. Jones and Ms. Smith with students

Research suggests that White perspectives and cultural ways of being are centered in many of our schools and presented as the norm. Not only does this perpetuate White children's lack of awareness about Black people, but it has a direct negative impact on Black children. It is certainly okay for Black children to learn about all cultures as they become culturally competent, but developmentally, children should learn about their own cultures first, or at the very least, simultaneously.

Revolutionary loving teachers *believe* that Black children have a culture and that this culture is valid and dynamic. They do not view Black children's ways of being as an aberration of White culture. They understand that an important first step to countering attacks on Black children's culture is to believe that there is such a thing as Black culture and to recognize it in Black children's interactions and behaviors.

PAUSE & REFLECT

▶ **Before reading the next section, jot down some things you know about Black culture.** How do you use this knowledge in your teaching and curriculum?

▶ **What do you believe about Black culture?**

What Do Revolutionary Loving Teachers KNOW?

Revolutionary loving ECE teachers know that:

1. **Black people are not acultural.** This means that Black cultural traditions, beliefs, and worldviews have been passed along cross-generationally. At the same time, Black culture, like other cultures, is dynamic and ever-evolving.

2. **Black culture includes implicit (attitudes, beliefs) and explicit (e.g., language, dress, music, religious rituals) aspects** (Boutte & DeFlorimonte, 1998).

3. **Black people have multiple identities, and there are many ways of being Black.** This means that Black children will perform their racial identities in different and in complicated ways. At the same time, Black people have a collective present, as well as historical experiences and memories, that cannot be overlooked or undermined (Boutte, 2022).

Researchers have identified 11 cultural dimensions unique to African culture (Boykin, 1994; Hale, 2001; Hale-Benson, 1986; Hilliard, 1992; King, 2005; Shade, 1997)—dimensions that represent *deep culture* and are common among people of African descent worldwide, though they reveal themselves in different ways. These dimensions should be viewed as strengths and legacies among Black children and families and can serve as important starting points for literacy and interdisciplinary engagement in ECE classrooms.

The 11 Cultural Dimensions

1. **SPIRITUALITY:** The belief in something greater than oneself

2. **HARMONY:** To live in relationship with all that is around us

3. **MOVEMENT:** An understanding of the importance of rhythm, music, and dance in one's life

4. **VERVE:** To feel that energetic action is an important component in life

5. **AFFECT:** An emphasis on emotions and feelings as well as sensitivity to the emotions and feelings of others

6. **COMMUNALISM:** A commitment to social connectedness and an awareness of social bonds

7. **EXPRESSIVE INDIVIDUALISM:** Spontaneous, genuine, joyful expression as part of a distinctive personality

8. **ORAL TRADITION:** The ability to use alliterative, metaphorically colorful and graphic forms of spoken language

9. **SOCIAL TIME PERSPECTIVE:** An orientation in which time is treated as passing through a social space and not a material one— the idea that time is a social construction

10. **PERSEVERANCE:** The ability to maintain a sense of agency and strength in the face of adversities

11. **IMPROVISATION:** The substitution of alternatives that are more sensitive to the nature of Black culture

While we sometimes talk about Black culture in general terms, there is, of course, variation among African American children. We know that revolutionary loving teachers will be able to make adaptations as needed for their own classroom. We may use the terms *African American* and *Black* interchangeably at times, but note that *Black* is more expansive. *Black* refers to Black people all over the globe (racially but not ethnically). *African American* specifically refers to Black people from the United States.

For simplicity, we've condensed the 11 dimensions into three core cultural practices: Harmony, Expression, and Communication. We think that considering these practices (and the underlying 11 dimensions they represent) can be a powerful way to incorporate children's lived experiences into the classroom. (For a detailed view of the 11 dimensions, see the Appendix.)

Three Core Practices Built on African American Culture

Cultural Practices	Believe	Know	Do
Harmony (includes Spirituality and Perseverance)	Something greater than oneself is essential and everything is connected.	Help students reflect on their life's purpose (why they exist), their gifts, their interests, and their goals. Help students connect to nature.	Directly teach relaxation, self-regulation techniques (e.g., meditation, belly breathing) to help students find calm and feel grounded and connected to themselves and others.
Expression (includes Oral Tradition, Movement, Verve, Expressive Individualism, Improvisation)	Creative expression is important.	Engage children in movement with music and dance. Allow space for children to creatively express themselves.	Bring in music and dance to classroom activities. Consider creating classroom rituals, such as cleanup time, that incorporate song and rhythm.
Communication (Affect, Communalism, Social Time Perspective)	Connectedness and goodness are guiding principles that help us recognize the good in each other and follow rules that model human goodness.	Integrate information about Black communities and sages and living history (e.g., regularly bring in elders and sages from the community).	Emphasize the South African principle, *Ubuntu* (I am because we are). Find time for including group work so that children learn to work together.

What Do Revolutionary Loving Teachers DO?

Now let's consider how to implement the three core practices in the classroom. What does it look like to make these cultural dimensions come alive?

Harmony

During our visits to West African countries, we've noticed tall termite mounds alongside residences and other buildings for humans. Apparently, when given a space to thrive, the termites have no need to bother the buildings. Both humans and termites coexist peacefully. This is an example of *harmony*.

Another striking example comes from a recent visit to Nigeria during the rainy season. We noticed that despite moderate rain, Nigerians carried on with their daily activities and walked about, some with umbrellas and some without. Rain seems to be accepted as a part of the life cycle and Nigerians move in concert with it instead of waiting for the rainfall to stop or rushing from buildings to modes of transportation. It was refreshing to watch.

Harmony is the notion that our lives and destinies are interrelated with other elements so that humankind and nature are harmonically conjoined. Educators who tap into this dimension help children connect to nature by involving them in outdoor activities. Making connections to historical and contemporary Black people who demonstrate strong connections with nature can be done by reading biographies and watching short videos about them.

Connections can be made by asking children for examples of people in their family who love plants, outdoors, fishing, and so forth. Over time, children can learn how there is a long history of African people connecting with nature. This value traveled with African people who were enslaved and was instrumental in the growth of crops and development of natural medicines. Contemporary examples can be seen when Black people pay attention to the signs of nature to know when storms are coming, seasons are changing, and much more. Here are two recommended books on the subject:

- Coombs, K. (2021). *Little Naturalists: George Washington Carver Loved Plants*. Babylit.

- Coombs, K. (2021). *Little Naturalists: Wangari Maathai Planted Trees*. Babylit.

Expression

Expression as a core practice includes the cultural dimensions of movement, verve, expressive individualism, and improvisation. While African Americans tend to be communal people, there is also room for individual expression, whether physically, socially, intellectually, linguistically, or emotionally. Here are a few examples. Ms. Collins, mentioned earlier, loves extremely large earrings. She is also known to have an air of sophistication evidenced in her careful and soft speech and blinking of her eyes when something is questionable. Each of us share examples of our distinctiveness below.

- Since Gloria was 14 years old, her hair has been some shade of red. Whether sporting an Afro, Afro puffs (as she did in the late 1970s), braids, crochets, or straight styles, her statement of distinction is her trademark red hair. She also likes *big* hair. Likewise, she prides herself on her wit and her smile, which also make her distinct.

- Kamania is known for always having a smile on her face. When she was teaching second grade, she remembers one of her students asking, with his own huge smile, "Ms. Wynter, why are you always smiling? Even when you are mad at us, you are smiling." She never thought about it until she was asked.

- Since he was 21 years old, Nathaniel has worn bow ties as a part of his professional wardrobe because he considers them a statement of distinction. His former students and colleagues often complimented him on his style of dress, and his Black male students often imitated his style by wearing bow ties during school events.

Some West African primary- and secondary-school teachers and administrators dress uniquely for special programs. They may choose a fabric with the same design, but each person has the fabric designed in a way that suits his or her particular style. Gloria also noticed this when she taught at a university in Nigeria. For group project presentations, students dressed in clothes made of the same fabric, but in different styles—one with a ruffled front, another with bell sleeves, some dresses flared, others straight. In other words, expressive individualism allows for unity *and* diversity.

Students at Labeo Comprehensive College in Lagos, Nigeria

Teachers who practice revolutionary love can capture and capitalize on Black children's expressive individualism by observing and/or asking them what makes them unique or special. When Ms. Collins taught first grade, she routinely created personalized books profiling all the children in her classroom in individual and collective ways. Ms. Collins's class books tapped into children's expression, while also serving as tools to teach literacy. These personalized books were read and reread—likely because the children themselves were featured in them. Using teacher-made books allowed children's literacy development and racial identities to be affirmed. Here are some examples of the books created in Ms. Collins's class.

Teacher-Created Class Books Highlighting Expression

Book Covers	Predictable Text	Content	Literacy Skills
School Is In By Ms. Saudah Collins Featuring the Scholars of Room 290	School is in! Look, here is our friend, _____.	Features students and their photos and names on individual pages	• repetition • predictable text • high-frequency words
It's Time for Lunch! Written by _____ Featuring _____	Eat, eat, eat. Munch, munch, munch! It's time for _____ to eat his lunch.	Presents students and their lunch choices	• onomatopoeia • rhyming words • predictable text • repetition

Book Covers	Predictable Text	Content	Literacy Skills
We Are First-Grade Scholars Written by Ms. S. Collins Photographs by Ms. C. Jimenez	Here's our friend, _____. That's her name. Without her our class would not be the same.	Highlights students and their photos and names	• rhyming phrases • repetition • high-frequency words • predictable text
We Love Our Hair Inspired by *I Love My Hair* by Natasha Tarpley Written by Ms. Saudah Collins Featuring the Scholars of 290	I love my hair. You can see. My _____ looks very nice on me. This is not the end. Turn the page to see my friend.	Celebrates children's hairstyles	• rhyming phrases • repetition • high-frequency words • predictable text
What's Your Hairstyle? Written by Ms. S. Collins & Ms. C. Jimenez	I have a _____ haircut (style). Can't you see? My _____ looks very nice on me! This is not the end. Turn the page to see my friend!	Presents a celebration of students and their hairstyles such as Afros, pony puffs, braids, and locs	• rhyming phrases • repetition • high-frequency words • predictable text
The Colors of Serena	Serena plays in a (color) outfit. Play, Serena, play!	Showcases Serena Williams in various colorful tennis outfits and her signature refrain, "Come on!"	• color words • high-frequency words • quotations marks • predictable text

Communication

Communication as a core practice includes the cultural dimensions of affect, communalism, and social time perspective. It is about helping children understand how they connect to themselves and others. Communication reflects a commitment to social connectedness, which includes an awareness that social bonds and responsibilities extend beyond the individual. Schools and U.S. society tend to value the rights and priorities of individual children and families over those of communities or groups. Black culture focuses on communication.

Communication as a core practice also includes the cultural dimension of *social time perspective*. This refers to an orientation in which time is treated as passing through a social space rather than a material one, and in which time can be recurring, personal, and phenomenological. Time is acknowledged as a social construct.

Trish Cooke's book, *So Much!,* contains a celebration for a father of the family. For years, Gloria has read the book to preservice and in-service teachers as a rich example of African American Language and family love. Before she reads, she explains that she bought the book in 1996 soon after her son, Jonathan, was born because she loved the imagery of a Black family doing things that her own family did—gathering and celebrating while engaged in a variety of activities such as playing games, eating, dancing, and just having fun. Gloria was particularly attracted to the image of a Black professional father, since that depiction of a father was/is often missing from children's

books. She loved the author's use of a form of African American Language from New Orleans (the birthplace of her children's father), which repeats adjectives for emphasis. For example, instead of saying that something is big, Jonathan's dad would say, *big, big, big yeah*. Gloria loved the affirmation of this language that the book captured. However, because Gloria was so embedded in Black culture, it wasn't until she was reading the book to a graduate class one day when one of her White male students asked, *What time was the party?* In the book, guests (family members) arrive at different times, which made sense to Gloria because in Black culture, time is a fluid construct. If a party begins at, say, seven o'clock, guests understand that to mean seven*ish* and will arrive around 7:30, 8:00, or later. This is an example of *social time perspective* (Boute, 2022), and it confused the White male student. The underlying assumption is that man-made conventions of time can be suspended. It is okay for people to arrive at a time that makes sense without being controlled by narrow conceptions of time. This is not unique to Black people. Most indigenous, Latine, and other groups also have similar notions.

This does not mean that teachers do not have to teach children to be cognizant of time at school and elsewhere. It does mean, however, that teachers need to understand the meaning of time from a Black cultural perspective. The idea of rushing around in a "timely" manner is a European cultural conception. When visiting countries in Africa, Gloria often reminds educators on study tours with her of this important insight so they will

not be in a hurry to be served quickly in restaurants or for events to move rapidly. Connecting with people and following natural body rhythms are more important than being a stickler for time—especially in informal settings. Teachers can engage students in discussions about how time is thought about in their families and communities.

PAUSE & REFLECT

▶ **What are some of your distinctive ways of expressing yourself?**

▶ **What examples of expressive distinctiveness have you noticed among the Black children in your classroom?**

Practices	Observations	Your Reflection/Examples
Harmony	Are Black children being encouraged to connect with nature through classroom activities?	
Expression	In what ways are Black children expressing their creative individualism? Are they encouraged to feel special and unique?	
Communication	Do children have a chance to build community with others within the classroom?	

Template available at scholastic.com/revlove-early-resources

What Can You DO NOW in the Classroom?

1. Choose one or two books that honor Black culture and read and discuss them with children.

2. As a part of your morning routine, include short affirmations that address Black cultural dimensions such as harmony, expression, and communication. Here is an example of a call and response affirmation created by Gloria Boutte and Janice Baines:

TEACHER: Who are you?

CHILDREN: I am a scholar!

TEACHER: What do scholars do?

CHILDREN: We love learning!

TEACHER: Why do you love learning?

CHILDREN: Because it is in my DNA from our ancestors and we are destined to achieve!

TEACHER: Ase! (which means "and so it is.")

Note: You may put your affirmation to a rhythm or borrow from a positive song like the Nas song "I Can."

What Can You DO IN THE UPCOMING WEEKS?

1. Continue to build your classroom library with relevant books. Consult our website at revlovebooks.com as well as scholastic.com/revlove-early-resources for book recommendations of quality children's literature that centers on the Black experience.

2. Read the books regularly, revisiting favorites from time to time (rather than reading them just once).

3. **Find songs that validate Black culture and share them with children.** Think of the many ways songs can support literacy—you might write out the lyrics so children can read as they sing along.

4. **Create books that reflect the culture of children in your classroom.** See examples of teacher-created books on pages 47–48.

What Can You DO BEYOND YOUR CLASSROOM?

1. **Ask families to share books or music that they read and listen to at home that reflect Black culture.**

2. **Either alone or with children, visit the media center in your center or school to see how many books address Black culture.** Make the case to your administrator for building a more diverse library or write a grant for new books of your choice.

3. **Ask administrators to schedule ongoing professional development on Black culture.**

4. **Read professional books and articles on Black culture.** Here are a couple to consider:

- "Hey, Black Child. Do you know who you are?" Using African diaspora literacy to humanize blackness in early childhood education, by Wynter-Hoyte, K., & Smith, M. *Journal of Literacy Research*, (2020). *52*(4), 406–431.

- Educating or imprisoning the spirit: Lessons from ancient Egypt, by Delpit, L., & White-Bradley, P. (2003). *Theory Into Practice, 42*(4), 283–288.

Chapter 3

CREATING SAFE, JOYFUL PLAY SPACES FOR CHILDREN

S HOW AND TELL IS NEKA'S FAVORITE PART OF THE DAY in Ms. Mackey's kindergarten class, when she and classmates share examples of activities and games they play at home. Neka has used this time and space to share jump-rope and hand-clap games. Her enthusiasm spills out of the classroom onto the yard, where, during recess time, she teaches other children how to play the games. Ms. Mackey has seen Neka leading children, of all ethnicities, through the hand-clap game *Miss Mary Mack*. While the children see the game as something fun and amusing, Ms. Mackey sees much more. She sees a diverse group of children engaged in cooperation as they practice onset and rime while hand-clapping and chanting, "Miss Mary Mack, Mack, Mack, all dressed in black, black, black."

What Do Revolutionary Loving Teachers BELIEVE?

Embracing revolutionary love in early childhood classrooms requires teachers to create safe and joyful play spaces for Black children. Ms. Mackey welcomes children's play literacies from home into her ECE classroom. Ms. Mackey has a deep appreciation for the strength and possibilities of Black children's play and creates safe, joyful learning spaces.

ECE teachers who embrace revolutionary love, like Ms. Mackey, believe that safe and joyful play spaces support the academic and social development of Black children. They believe that play is an essential part of children's growth that leads to positive outcomes, and it should never be restricted or denied as punishment for Black children. They understand that the core practice of *expression* means that children need opportunities for joyful play.

Young children who have access to play are more likely to perform academically and socially better than their peers who have limited access to play (Souto-Manning & Martell, 2017). Yet, research shows that Black children, unlike their White counterparts, are not often afforded safe and joyful play spaces in early childhood classrooms and beyond. Early childhood teachers often restrict Black children's physical movements and activities, or see Black children's play as problematic and, as such, in need of modification. For example, Nathaniel recalls how his teachers often summoned his classmates and him to "stand against the wall," during recess, which served as an exclusionary form of discipline to correct "misbehavior" (e.g., talking during class, failing to complete assignments, and breaking classroom rules and expectations). Such forms of discipline are acts of physical violence, which also negatively impact children academically, socially, and psychologically (Boutte & Bryan, 2021; Bryan 2018, 2020, 2021).

Students exhibiting Black joy

Knowing that play is an integral part of childhood education, teachers who embrace revolutionary love believe Black children should have access to safe and joyful play spaces.

What Do Revolutionary Loving Teachers KNOW?

ECE teachers who embrace revolutionary love understand the history of Black children's play experiences and how it informs Black children's present and future play experiences. During the enslavement of African people, Black children were often denied opportunities to play and, instead, worked alongside their parents in rice and cotton fields (Bryan, 2020; Perry et al., 2003). When Black children were granted opportunities for play, they sometimes played with White children and learned to read and write English from them, which they in turn taught their enslaved parents. As such, their play sometimes served as an act of freedom. One might say, when White children were freely playing, Black children were playing for freedom. Today we continue to see freedom of play available more to White children than Black children. Black children are often punished for infractions that White children are not. When teachers become knowledgeable about how Black children's play has been restricted historically, they are less likely to repeat the past and instead make play available equally to all children.

Another problem is that Black children are often *adultified* (seen as adults rather than children). A study from Georgetown Law Center on Poverty and Inequality revealed that Black girls are seen as less innocent and more adult-like than their White peers between the age range of 5 and 14. By age 10, Black boys are more likely than their White peers to be perceived as older, and more likely to encounter police violence if accused of a crime (Goff et al., 2014). Since we know that schools reflect society at large, we should not be surprised that Black boys make up 18 percent of the male preschool enrollment but 41 percent of male preschool suspensions, and Black girls make up 19 percent of female preschool enrollment but account for 53 percent of female suspensions.

One reason for this problem might be that Black children are often watched in anticipation of negative behaviors. Dr. Walter Gilliam and colleagues at the Yale Childhood Center (2016) found that teachers held negative views and misperceptions of Black children's play styles and behaviors in early childhood classrooms. During the study, teachers watched a video of White and Black children playing and were asked to identify misbehavior. Although Dr. Gilliam and colleagues had suggested that there was no evidence of misbehavior among the children in the video, the majority of the teachers, both Black and White, identified misbehavior among the Black children. In other words, the teachers anticipated misbehavior from Black students and labeled their mundane behaviors accordingly. Black children also internalize such negative and deficit perceptions.

Traumatic Play Experiences of Black Children in Early Childhood Classrooms

Despite the importance of childhood play, research suggests that some early childhood teachers criminalize the play styles of Black children, albeit unintentionally in most cases. That behavior limits Black children's access to play and recreation, causes psychological trauma, and negatively impacts their academic and social skills (Bryan, 2018; 2021). Take, for example, the experience of a nine-year-old Black boy, Bryce Lindley. Bryce was playing an innocent game of dodgeball with a nine-year-old White boy. During the game, Bryce hit the boy with the ball, which typically happens during such a game. Bryce was suspended from school, and later charged with aggravated assault (Bryan et al., 2022; Elliot, 2019). White children often engage in similar mishaps during play, yet their behaviors are often met with less harsh consequences. When Nathaniel served as an assistant principal in a predominantly White magnet elementary school in South Carolina, a White student assaulted a Black student during a basketball game. The White student's behavior was not addressed. Instead, the supervisor told Nathaniel,

"It was just a mistake." However, research suggests that Black children are often not perceived to "just be making mistakes" but are often criminalized on and off the school playground (Bryan, 2021; Milner & Tenore, 2010).

Another area of concern is how Black children play in the classroom and the roles they are assigned. Dr. Rachel Rosen (2017) conducted a study on children's play in a preschool setting and found that the antagonistic roles, such as monster or villain, that children assumed during play experiences remained "stuck" to the Black children's bodies long after the play experience ended, yet when White children assumed the antagonistic roles during play, they were able to shake those roles from their bodies immediately after their play experiences. This is particularly disturbing considering that we've seen many examples of elementary Black children assigned to act as enslaved people during school activities. For example, during "Civil War Day" in a school in Georgia, one Black child was told by his White classmate, "You are my slave" (Martin, 2017). This type of casting during class forces Black children to assume and carry the weight of a racially inferior role as a "slave" with White children playing cruel and unjust figures such as "slave masters."

Kindergarten children learning through play

Contrary to popular belief, young children do see race, as early as three months old (Kelly et al., 2005). Children from all racial backgrounds will internalize racial messages through play. Take, for example, Studio Kids Little River Preschool in Miami, Florida, where the two-year-olds in the classroom wore Blackface to "celebrate" Black History Month. Teachers, Blackface is never a good idea! Blackface performances are historically rooted in racist messages to stereotype and demoralize Black people. What messages were these non-Black children receiving about Black people? That Black people are caricatures, which they can put on and take off at their own free will. As educators, we have to question, think critically about, and lovingly wonder about the impact of play on the psyche of Black children, as well as the messages of superiority White children are learning through play.

They're Not Too Young to Talk About Race

Young children notice and think about race. Adults often worry that talking about race will encourage racial bias in children, but the opposite is true. Silence about race reinforces racism by letting children draw their own conclusions based on what they see. Teachers and families can play a powerful role in helping children of all ages develop positive attitudes about race and diversity and skills to promote a more just future—but only if we talk about it.

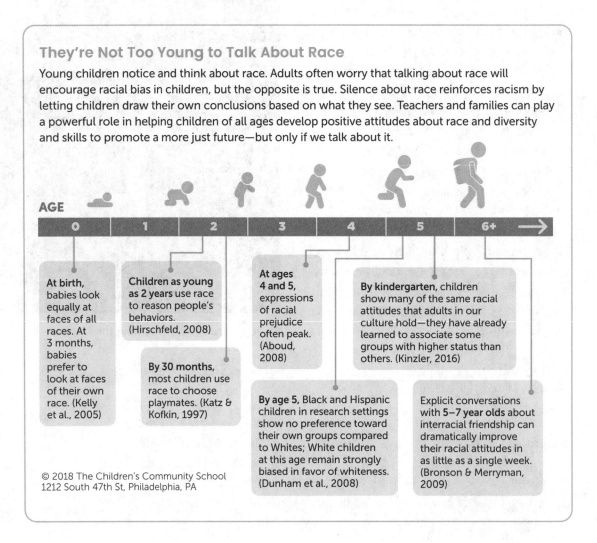

AGE 0 1 2 3 4 5 6+ →

At birth, babies look equally at faces of all races. At 3 months, babies prefer to look at faces of their own race. (Kelly et al., 2005)

Children as young as 2 years use race to reason people's behaviors. (Hirschfeld, 2008)

By 30 months, most children use race to choose playmates. (Katz & Kofkin, 1997)

At ages 4 and 5, expressions of racial prejudice often peak. (Aboud, 2008)

By age 5, Black and Hispanic children in research settings show no preference toward their own groups compared to Whites; White children at this age remain strongly biased in favor of whiteness. (Dunham et al., 2008)

By kindergarten, children show many of the same racial attitudes that adults in our culture hold—they have already learned to associate some groups with higher status than others. (Kinzler, 2016)

Explicit conversations with **5–7 year olds** about interracial friendship can dramatically improve their racial attitudes in as little as a single week. (Bronson & Merryman, 2009)

© 2018 The Children's Community School
1212 South 47th St, Philadelphia, PA

Revolutionary Love for Early Childhood Classrooms

Let's Explore Kamania's Childhood Experience

I wished that my teachers recognized and honored my play as Ms. Mackey did in the opening scenario. As a Black girl, born to immigrant parents, raised in Brooklyn and later South Florida, I was surrounded by many literacies and multiple languages. While playing with my sisters and friends, I remember the sounds of reggae music as our soundtrack in the background. The adults in the home would sing along to songs that called for human rights and liberation.

I developed close-knit friendships with children from different ethnic backgrounds. As a guest in their homes, I understood how to adapt to other norms and traditions according to their cultures. My peers would model appropriate play behaviors, such as making sure that I turned over my teacup to be filled; and at another friend's, when playing house, we would greet each other with a kiss on each cheek.

Play outdoors centered around a jump rope, where we would chant rhymes that aligned with the beat of the rope. As we got older, we would play double Dutch. I successfully navigated the complexities of my community but failed in school. Where was the disconnect between my school and community? And more importantly, how do we get teachers to honor the types of play and funds of knowledge children already have? Kyra Gaunt (2020) addresses many of these questions in her *New York Times* piece, "The Magic of Black Girls' Play." In it, she states, "we miss the way Black girls often enter the classroom with their own forms of teaching and learning, from hand-clapping game-songs to jumping rope." She continues, "games are a way for Black girls to learn how social relationships are negotiated and rooted in African culture"

Before moving on to the next sections, we invite you to reflect on the following questions:

PAUSE & REFLECT

▶ In what ways have you unintentionally misperceived/misjudged Black children's play?

▶ Have you ever withheld the opportunity to play as a punishment for a Black child?

▶ What can you do to work against your personal misperceptions of Black children's play?

▶ How can you begin to affirm Black children's play?

Observing Black Children's Play

Practices	Observations	Your Reflection
Perceived misbehavior	Preconceived notions making educators "see" what isn't really there.	
Adultification	Are Black children treated in a way that aligns with their ages?	
Access to play spaces	Do Black children have access to safe and joyful play spaces? Is play restricted as a form of punishment?	
Role-Play	Are Black children assigned positive roles for role-play and reenactments?	
Home Play Literacies	Are students encouraged to share games from home with their classmates?	

Template available at scholastic.com/revlove-early-resources

What Do Revolutionary Loving Teachers DO?

In the chart below, we outline what ECE teachers believe, know, and do to create safe, joyful learning play spaces for Black children.

Teachers' Beliefs, Knowledge, and Actions About Black Children's Play		
Believe	**Know**	**Do**
Teachers who embrace revolutionary love believe that Black children desire the right to play in safe and joyful spaces. They are committed to contesting the physical violence that impedes Black children's play.	Teachers who embrace revolutionary love must know the history of Black children's play and understand how *adultification* can create unsafe and joyless play spaces for Black children.	Teachers who embrace revolutionary love foster Black children's play by providing a space that is always safe and joyful.

What Can You DO NOW in the Classroom?

1. **Ask children to share their favorite games with the class.** Carve out a regular time and space for this sharing.

2. **Observe Black children playing during recess or free time.** What do you notice? Focus not only on what you can learn *about* Black children's play, but also what you can learn *from* it. Do you have any misconceptions or deficit views that you need to reconsider?

What Can You DO IN THE UPCOMING WEEKS?

1. **Integrate texts (e.g., videos, films, posters, toys, video games, sports) that offer strength-based perspectives on Black culture.**

2. **Use read-alouds to begin a study of African games.** The following books by Nigerian author Ifeoma Onyefulu celebrate children's play.

- ***Ebele's Favourite: A Book of African Games*** This book shows games that African children play and can serve as windows for Black children to understand similarities and differences of play among African-descendant people.

- ***Look at This! Play*** This book also shows African children playing in everyday, routine ways. It captures the idea of Black children simply being children.

- ***Omer's Favorite Place*** This book is about a young African boy who engages in a game of finding favorite places in his home. It shows the global aspect of common games children play; thus, it humanizes African children (rather than depicting them as "poor" children in need of missionaries to save them).

3. **Add books to your classroom library that feature children at play.** Review the books below and consider adding them to your classroom library. These titles do double duty by fitting into the three core practices (harmony, expression, and communication).

Books That Serve as Mirrors for *Harmony*

***Come On, Rain!* by Karen Hesse** This book recreates the body and soul-renewing experience of a summer downpour after a sweltering city heat wave. Through exquisite language and acute observation, it recreates the glorious experience of a quenching rainstorm on a sweltering summer day.

Mia Mayhem series by Kara West Mia Macarooney, an ordinary eight-year-old, finds out she has an extraordinary super-secret! She experiences awesome adventures as she enrolls in a top-secret superhero academy, learns to fly, races against a super bully, and figures out how to control her super strength!

***The Year We Learned To Fly* by Jacqueline Woodson** "Use those beautiful and brilliant minds of yours. Lift your arms, close your eyes, take a deep breath, and believe in a thing." This book celebrates the extraordinary ability to lift ourselves up and imagine a better world.

Books That Serve as Mirrors for *Expression*

***Max Found Two Sticks* by Brian Pinkney**
Max picks up the sticks and begins tapping out the rhythms of everything he sees and hears around him—the sound of pigeons startled into flight, of rain against the windows, of distant church bells and the rumble of a subway. And then, when a marching band rounds Max's corner, something wonderful happens. Brian Pinkney's rhythmic text and lively pictures are certain to get many a child's foot tapping, many a youngster drumming.

***I Got the Rhythm* by Connie Schofield-Morrison** On a simple trip to the park, the joy of music overtakes a mother and daughter. The little girl hears a rhythm coming from the world around her—from butterflies to street performers to ice cream sellers, everything is musical!

Books That Serve as Mirrors for *Communication*

***Our People* by Angela Shelf Medearis**
A child and father playfully explore great moments of African American history, from the heritage of Black rulers to Black cowboys and inventors. Lively text and glowing illustrations fill young Black readers with a pride in and new understanding of their heritage.

***Tar Beach* by Faith Ringgold** Faith Ringgold weaves fiction, autobiography, and African American history into a magical story that resonates with the universal wish for freedom, and will be cherished for generations.

What Can You DO BEYOND YOUR CLASSROOM?

1. **In collaboration with administrators, examine disciplinary policies and practices to determine if Black children's play is being profiled and penalized at your school.** Change policies and practices as necessary.

2. **Invite adult Black family members to your class to share games they played as children.**

Chapter 4

EMBRACING THE BEAUTY AND POWER OF AFRICAN AMERICAN LANGUAGE

Revolutionary Love for Early Childhood Classrooms

W HEN FIRST GRADER KWAME WAS READING ALOUD to Meagan, a preservice teacher working with him, he pronounced the word *that* as *dat*. Meagan excitedly responded, "Yes! Did you know that when you said '*dat*,' you were speaking a beautiful language called African American Language? Let's look at the word again. In Standard English, how would we read it? Look at the beginning sound. Yes, it's 'th'— *that*. Do you know what you just did? You translated that word in your brain from one language to another. That's brilliant! And do you know what else? Parts of African American Language come from beautiful languages of West Africa, where people use a 'd' sound and not a 'th' sound. Cool, isn't it? Let's write the words in both languages."

What Do Revolutionary Loving Teachers BELIEVE?

In the opening scenario, it is clear that Meagan believed that Kwame's pronunciation of the word *that* was valid. She believed that children naturally translate Standard English (SE) into the language they learn at home. She demonstrated that it is important to validate children's language, while also teaching them other languages or dialects. Meagan had learned about African American Language in her teacher preparation program and, therefore, was able to validate Kwame's language and acknowledge his brilliance. She also pointed out to Kwame that *dat* is another legitimate way to pronounce *that*. Because the exchange occurred during a read-aloud and the other children could hear it, they learned that Kwame was smart and that both AAL and SE pronunciations are valid.

ECE teachers who embrace revolutionary love believe that children's language is intimately tied to their cultural and familial identities. The home languages that children bring to educational settings are ones they have been learning since birth. They are the languages they will use to express themselves best and the ones they feel most comfortable using. Revolutionary loving teachers embrace and validate home languages. They know that in order to add Standard English to their linguistic repertoire, they have to view home languages as valid, strong, and rule-governed. They do not police students' home languages, but rather embrace them for their beauty and sophistication—and use them as a powerful foundation for language development.

Since Hart and Risley's study came out in 1992, many educators and policymakers have been influenced by the findings indicating that, by age three, children living in poverty were exposed to 30 million fewer words than affluent children. However, researchers have since found that the study was flawed for a variety of reasons, including a small sample size of 42 families, a strong bias of race and class, and a deficit view of "fixing" the language of low socioeconomic families and children of color (Sperry, Sperry & Miller, 2019). For some educators, this study suggested that children's home languages were not as valued as Standard English. African American Language has been a particular point of focus with some educators believing that it is not a language to be valued in the school setting.

What Do Revolutionary Loving Teachers KNOW?

Like Kwame's teacher, who understood that his pronunciation of the word *that* during read-aloud reflected his home language, teachers who embrace revolutionary love know that African American Language (AAL) is a legitimate form of speech with a rich historical basis.

You may have heard AAL referred to by many other names such as "Black English," "African American English," "Black English Vernacular," "Ebonics," and "African American Vernacular English," to name a few. AAL refers to the language system characteristically spoken in the African American community.

Revolutionary loving teachers acknowledge that African American students are not monolithic and note that some of them speak Standard English (SE) as their first language. Black children who speak SE as their home language may tend to assimilate and not encounter linguistic violence and discrimination in the classroom. This violence occurs when Black children are constantly corrected for speaking AAL and eventually silenced in the classroom (Delpit, 2012) or when instructional programs encourage children to code switch from AAL to SE (Wheeler, Swords, & Carpenter, 2004). These misconceptions of AAL also lead to the over-referral of African American children in special education (Gold & Richards, 2012) based on language deficiencies. We also must consider the kind of damaging messages Black families are receiving about their home language and essentially their identities. This deficit way of thinking about AAL alienates Black families from schools and strains parent-school relationships. Yet, 80–90 percent of African American children speak AAL as their first language (Perry & Delpit, 1998) and we consider what this means for teaching and assessing Black children who do speak AAL. Black children who do not speak AAL as their first language and children from other ethnic groups benefit from learning that AAL is a legitimate way of communicating and that there is nothing wrong with AAL or the children who speak it. They won't learn this if AAL is silenced and "corrected" in classrooms on a daily basis (Delpit, 2012; Souto-Manning, 2009). Texts and conversations around AAL need to play a prominent role in classroom libraries and read-alouds.

AAL is a legitimate systematic language that follows a clear set of linguistic rules (Linguistic Society of America, 1997; Smitherman, 1977/1985; 2000; 2001; 2006). The term *AAL* acknowledges the relationship to West African languages.

The research around AAL suggests four key points:

1. **No language is better or worse than any other language** (Boutte, 2016; Souto-Manning, 2010).

2. **AAL is a rule-governed language.** For instance, the double negative syntactic feature (e.g., "don't have no") is often frowned upon but is a common feature deemed beautiful and admired when used in French and numerous other languages.

3. **As educators, we are not teaching students how to speak AAL.** They already know how to speak AAL—we are simply adding SE to their linguistic repertoires.

4. **Students have a right to use their own language** (Baugh, 2015; Kinloch, 2005; Smitherman, 2001), and it is our job as educators to help them add SE to their existing language repertoires, without trying to eradicate or demean their first language and the language of their mothers (Boutte & Johnson, 2012, 2013; Boutte, 2016; Souto-Manning, 2010).

Please see the Appendix for a detailed description of the features and rules that characterize AAL, contrasted with those of SE. The chart summarizes some of what we know about AAL from more than five decades of academic literature on the topic.

▶ Take a moment to reflect on how you respond to African American Language speakers. Note: You may also know AAL as Ebonics, African American English, or other similar terms, or may think of it as "incorrect" English.

PAUSE & REFLECT

▶ Complete the template below to gauge your typical reactions to AAL. This activity will be useful as you move ahead on your journey to revolutionary teaching because it will help you identify your thoughts about AAL that you may or may not be aware of. There is no judgment and what you write is for your eyes only and in the interest of advancing revolutionary love in your classroom.

Your Reactions to AAL

What the student said	Your Response—did you: cringe; "correct" the student; affirm the student/offer a compliment; say nothing, etc.?	Reflect on your response

Adapted with permission from Wynter-Hoyte, Braden, Myers, Rodriguez, & Thornton (2022)
Template available at scholastic.com/revlove-early-resources

What Do Revolutionary Loving Teachers DO?

Revolutionary loving teachers find ways to validate children's home languages and center curriculum around those languages. One way they do that is by normalizing the geographical, historical, and cultural background of AAL before exploring the language itself. Below are a few preK–1 classroom examples of how teachers respect the languages that children bring to class.

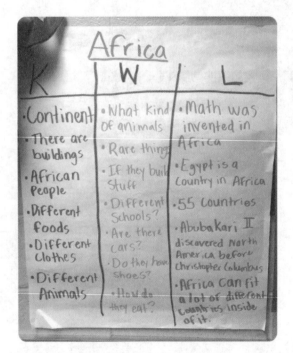

A bulletin board display of Ms. Mukkaramah Smith's first-grade class, after completing a unit on Africa. The children learned about Africa's contributions to the world and participated in an interactive writing activity after learning about Mansa Musa.

Ms. Mevelyn Gaither, a cross-grade Reading Interventionist teacher for the Center for the Education and Equity of African American Students (CEEAAS) learned that African American Language (AAL) was a legitimate, rules-governed language, and decided to revolutionize her teaching to better honor AAL. Seeking to create a healing and empowering space for young learners, Ms. Gaither cocreated a word wall with her students that included

AAL translations for high-frequency and other vocabulary words. In this way, AAL speakers understand that their language is legitimate and can reference the word wall using their natural pronunciations when trying to approximate conventional spellings.

A preschool or kindergarten word wall could include pictures of high-frequency words with both conventional and AAL spellings. Children can be taught that there are different ways of pronouncing words. For example, one way is in African American Language (e.g., *toof*) and another way is Standard English (*tooth*).

Ms. Gaither's student-generated word wall was a hit and students referenced it regularly when trying to spell words.

Ms. Gaither's Inclusive AAL Word Wall

The first-grade students will travel to the State Museum on November 29.

Cost: $10 • Due: November 20

The cost includes the field trip and the field trip T-shirt. Field trip T-shirts will be kept at school until the end of the school year.

THIS WEEK AT A GLANCE

Using African American Language and Standard English

The students will learn how to translate African American Language into Standard English in order to foster success.

Language Arts

Blending Words: *wh, w*

Ms. Collins' "Week at a Glance" Flyer

Not all teachers experience such buy-in when it comes to including AAL in the classroom. For example, when first-grade teacher Ms. Saudah Collins sent her weekly newsletter to families, which prominently featured "Using African American Language" as a goal of the week, she was surprised to receive this email from an African American mother: "I thought we as Black Americans was speaking English, but if not what are we speaking do enlighten me because I feel a little offended by this week's at a glance." Notwithstanding the parent's' use of an African American Language feature "...we **was** speaking," the parent's sentiments are not atypical when African American Language is mentioned. Most people do not recognize AAL as a rules-governed language.

Although Ms. Collins offered to meet with the parent several times, the parent never responded. Then, the following year, Ms. Collins began teaching all K–5 students in the school in a required African Studies course. This course was introduced after the principal and some of the teachers realized that even in their majority African American school, children were not learning anything about African descendant history and culture. In the African studies class, Ms. Collins had the same child in her class again. Ms. Collins heard from the parent again, but this time the parent wrote about her son's blossoming confidence about being Black and his enthusiasm for all he was learning. The parent emailed Ms. Collins to express her joy.

Blessed uprising Ms. Collins this is _____ mom . I would love to say thank you for teaching the African studies course in Jackson Creek. It gives _____ such pride within himself. _____ has taught me African dialect greetings, places in Africa. I see _____ absorbs a lot of information from this class he recites everything he has learned about Africa and African American history. Please can you cover Shamba Bolongongo the Congo king of peace. _____ birthday is this month so a shine on the 93rd Congo king Shamba would be great. That is _____ Middle name. Call me _____. (parent's name)

The parent's comments punctuate some of the benefits of teaching Black children from a cultural perspective. The comments reveal deeply held values, like those attached to names, which this teacher might not have otherwise discovered. African American children's language is a key part of Black culture and needs to be recognized as such in the classroom.

When we respect African American Language as parallel to Standard English or any other variations of it, we view both languages as legitimate languages that follow their respective linguistic rules. Understanding that AAL follows a set of rules for sounds, grammar, meanings, and social use (Alim & Smitherman, 2012; Boutte, 2007; Baugh, 1999; Linguistic Society of America, 1997; Rickford, 1999; Smitherman, 1977/1985; Smitherman, 2006) is foundational to honoring the linguistic brilliance of AAL.

Another feature of AAL is signifying. According to Geneva Smitherman, renowned sociolinguist and expert on AAL (2006), *signifying* is a "style of verbal play in which a speaker puts down; needles; or talks about a person, event, situation, or even a government. It depends on double meaning and irony, exploits the unexpected, and uses quick verbal surprises and humor. Signifying can be used for playful commentary or serious social critique, couched as play" (p. 43). The lineage of signifying has been traced to the trickster archetype found in African folklore. The trickster is known for playing tricks and disobeying rules and societal norms. We can see signifying on display in the children's book *Flossie and the Fox* (McKissack, 1986), which is written in AAL. Each time the fox tries to convince Flossie, the main character, that he is who he says he is, Flossie retorts with a quick, sassy remark. When teachers incorporate this kind of literature into their classrooms, they teach students to appreciate the beauty of AAL. During a read-aloud of *Flossie and the Fox*, students can hear the similarities of their home language to the language of the text. Teachers who start where children are with the language they bring from home and help them add Standard English and other languages to their repertoires (without seeking to erase their first languages), raise the chances of those children becoming bilingual (able to speak AAL and SE) and biliterate (be conversant in both AAL and SE literacies (Boutte & Johnson, 2012; 2013).

Center AAL in the Early Childhood Classroom

There are many ways to bring AAL into the classroom to model that all home languages should be honored. Role-playing is an easy way to help children practice using both languages (AAL and SE). When Kamania was a first-grade teacher, she gathered the students on the carpet and said, "In order for me to get this teaching position, I had to interview with Dr. Jones (the principal). Today I am going to show you three different greetings and I want you to tell me which one you think I did for the interview." Kamania walked out of the classroom and each time she entered she would speak a different language:

1. **African American Language:** "Hey, what up, Dr. Jones." She gestures giving the principal a dap. "What it do?", while clapping her hands. "I appreciate ya doin this interview and all, good lookin out."

2. **Standard English:** "Hello, good afternoon, Dr. Jones." She pretends to give the principal a handshake. "How are you doing today? Thanks for taking the time to interview me for the teaching position."

3. **Jamaican Patois:** "Wah gwaan, Dr. Jones!" She gestures giving the principal a hug. "Everyting criss. I apprecialove da interview, sistren."

After the role-play, Kamania engaged the class in a conversation about language. Many of the students stated that Kamania spoke using Standard English during the interview. She then confided that she used both Jamaican Patois (an English-based language spoken primarily in Jamaica with West African influences) and Standard English (literacy scholars refer to this as translanguaging or code-meshing, which means moving in and out of multiple languages). She explained that midway through the interview she realized her principal was a *yardie*, a term that refers to people of Jamaican origin; and how she connected with Dr. Jones by speaking a language the two are familiar with. In addition, she described that she started the interview in Standard English because that is deemed the language of power. This dramatic play in a first-grade classroom sparked an exploration of what AAL is, the power of language, and loving the languages we speak while learning how to be multilingual—we can teach children how to speak more than one language, and we can honor multiple languages while mastering SE. It does not have to be one or the other.

Take a moment to listen to Dr. Jamila Lyiscott, Assistant Professor of Social Justice Education at the University of Massachusetts Amherst, orator, and scholar activist, as she unpacks the three distinct flavors of speaking English. You may find her Ted Talk by searching the Internet using these keywords: "Jamila Lyiscott Trilingualism."

What Can You DO NOW in the Classroom?

1. **Stop "correcting" children's AAL:** When children speak or write in AAL, always allow fluency first, which means letting children express their ideas uninterrupted. As they expand their biliteracy and bilingualism, they can translate AAL to SE and edit as necessary. None of this should be done in a stilted, perfunctory way that discourages the child. This means that caution should be taken not to over-police the language of AAL speakers.

Scenario: A preschool child sharing excitement with a teacher in an informal, one-on-one conversation about his new dog

JAMAL: We got a new dawg yesterday. He have big ears.....

TEACHER: (after allowing Jamal to finish his story) That is wonderful. I love the way you told that story. When you said, *He have big ears*, I see you know how to speak African American Language well. (Here the teacher focuses on one linguistic feature—subject-verb agreement—so as not to overwhelm the child). Remember we talked about how you can say things more than one way? Do you know how to translate that sentence to Standard English? (The teacher gives the child time to respond. If the child does not know, the teacher can tell him: *He HAS big ears*.)

As teachers help AAL speakers develop bilingualism (proficiency in both AAL and SE), it will be important to avoid "correcting" AAL. Rather, teachers can help children develop linguistic versatility by translating from SE to AAL and AAL to SE, and not privileging SE over AAL. It is also important not to categorize AAL as *informal* language and SE as *formal*. As children learn to *translanguage* (use a mixture of AAL and SE), they develop as biliterates and bilinguals. Consult Rebecca Wheeler and Rachel Swords' *Code-Switching: Teaching Standard English in Urban Classrooms* (2006), for examples of strategies for helping children translate AAL to SE. Also, remember to spend time helping children translate SE into AAL.

2. **Keep a "Listen and Learn Notebook":** Write down examples of things that AAL speakers in your classroom say or write. Keep a record of these examples and look for language patterns. This will provide insight regarding the rules of AAL. It is not necessary to know the linguistic names of the features (e.g., *phonology*; *syntax*). Just write down examples and try to figure out the underlying rules (e.g., verb tense remains the same across first, second, and third person—*I is; You is; he/she/it is; we is; they is*). There will be times when you are unsure whether the examples represent AAL. Not to worry. It will take time and research to identify some features. The important thing is recognizing that AAL is not haphazard or incorrect English.

You may start with looking for some of the examples you wrote down on the template (p. 71). Then you may record some of those examples on a chart like the one on the following page. The chart shows examples that a teacher recorded after learning about AAL and listening carefully to AAL speakers. She was able to use what she now recognized as AAL to help students translate from AAL to SE.

Community member reading to students

Examples of AAL in My Classroom

Examples of each AAL linguistic feature from AAL speakers and/or writers in my classroom.

Sounds and Pronunciations	Grammar	Changing Meanings of Words	Vocabulary	Social Use of Language
Phonology: Sound system	**Syntax:** Rules for combining words into acceptable phrases, clauses, and sentences	**Morphology:** Rules for combining sounds into basic units of meaning (words)—e.g., how you make a word past tense, present tense, plural, possessive	**Semantics:** The meanings of individual words and word relationships in messages	**Pragmatics:** The function of language in social contexts including styles of speaking
Tes (test) Wuz (was) Wid, wit, (with) Goin' Workin' Fine (find)	What speakers mean?	Sawd (saw) Look lookded (Looked)	She stay workin' (she's always working) Dawg (dog)	

3. **Role-play:** Look for opportunities where you and your students can explore language through role-playing, similar to Kamania's job-interview example on page 76.

What Can You DO IN THE UPCOMING WEEKS?

1. **Cocreate a Classroom "Word Wall"** As you listen to AAL pronunciations that children use, keep a record of them and use them to create personalized word walls.

2. **Book "Talk"** An engaging way to begin conversations about AAL as a language system with your children is with books written with AAL-speaking narrators or characters. You may do so using texts written in AAL like the ones in the chart on pages 82–83. It may be useful to use prerecorded video readings to capture the nuances of AAL that non-AAL speakers may miss. *Sankofa Read Alouds* has many prerecorded read-alouds. As you and the children listen to the story, also note aspects of Black culture mentioned earlier (e.g., communalism, movement, orality).

To demonstrate that AAL is used by a wide variety of people, read or listen to an assortment of male and female characters set in different geographic contexts (e.g., urban, suburban, and rural settings). Likewise, try to choose books across different genres—e.g., fairy/folktales and realistic fiction. Be intentional about your selections (Boutte, 2015).

An early childhood preservice teacher instructing some of the phonetic rules discovered in a read-aloud with a kindergarten student

As students are reading or being read to, teachers and students can write down examples from the books translated into SE so children can see parallels. An important process in helping AAL speakers become biliterate (AAL and SE) is to give them oral and written opportunities to translate back and forth in explicit ways.

Examples of Read-Alouds Written in AAL

Read-alouds of these books are available on YouTube.

Book Title	Recommended Grade/Age Level	Summary
Flossie and the Fox (McKissack, 1986)	PreK–3rd	In this reimagining of the Little Red Riding Hood tale, Flossie comes across a mischievous fox while on her way to deliver a basket of eggs to her neighbor. However, the courageous and resourceful Flossie is determined to outwit him. After all, "a fox be just a fox."
The Black Snowman (Mendez, 1989)	2nd–5th	When a black snowman comes to life through the power of a magical kente cloth, young Jacob uncovers the profound beauty of his Black heritage and ancestry, fostering self-love and acceptance along the way.
Willie Jerome (Duncan, 1995)	1st and 2nd	Willie Jerome's summer jazz melodies fill the vibrant streets of Harlem; yet, their beauty often goes unnoticed by all but his sister Judy. Determined to sway Mama and the rest of the neighborhood, Judy sets out on a mission to help others celebrate and appreciate the significance of Willie's music.
'Twas the Night B'fore Christmas (Rosales, 1996)	1st and 2nd	This retelling of the classic holiday poem in African American Language follows a Black family as they excitedly await the arrival of Santy Claus.

Book Title		Recommended Grade/Age Level	Summary
	Working Cotton (Williams, 1997)	PreK–3rd	Told from the perspective of young Shelan, this book captures a day in the life of a Black family working in the cotton fields. Shelan helps her parents from sunrise to sundown, vividly describing the landscape and recognizing the effort that goes into sustaining their family.
	Bibbity Bop Barbershop (Tarpley, 2009)	PreK–3rd	In this book that celebrates a significant moment in the life of a young Black boy, Miles successfully braves his very first haircut at the local barbershop.
	Yo! Yes? (Raschka, 2007)	PreK–2nd	Making new friends doesn't need to require many words. Through a casual exchange of "Yo!" and "Yes?", two young boys embrace their differences and spark a connection that blossoms into a friendship.
	Don't Say Ain't (Smalls, 2004)	1st–4th	Set in the 1950s, Dana struggles to balance between her Harlem neighborhood and the integrated advanced school she attends, where she's expected to maintain "proper" speech. As she navigates both worlds, she strives to stay true to herself and her roots.
	Honey Baby Sugar Child (Duncan, 2005)	3–6 years	In this heartwarming tribute to the bond between a Black mother and her son, the moments they share— whether playing or cuddling—radiate warmth and illustrate the deep love present in a parent-child relationship.

Contrastive Analysis for *Flossie and the Fox*

AAL Examples	SE Translations
I <u>be</u> Flossie Finley.	I am Flossie Finley.
I reckon I don't know who you <u>be</u> either.	I guess I don't know who you are, either.
<u>You a rat</u> trying to pass <u>yo'self</u> off as a fox.	You are a rat trying to pass yourself off as a fox.
That still <u>don't</u> make you <u>no</u> fox.	That still doesn't make you a fox.

Contrastive Analysis for *Honey Baby Sugar Child*

AAL Examples	SE Translations
Honey baby, sugar child	Sweetie
I'm gone always be yo sweet Ma'Dear, and you gone always be my baby.	I will always be your sweet grandmother and you are always going to be my baby.
yo	your
I see them cheeks, them eyes…	I see those cheeks, those eyes…
You my favorite patty cake.	You are my favorite child.
You the star in my crown.	You are like a star in a crown.

What Can You DO BEYOND YOUR CLASSROOM?

1. **Find out more about the appropriateness of language assessments used in your setting.** Policy and assessment changes should accompany the goal of honoring AAL. Look for assessments that are culturally relevant and don't penalize students for using AAL. One example is the Diagnostic Evaluation of Language Variation™ (DELV) published by Ventris Learning. It differentiates between a language disorder, developmental delay, and dialect.

2. **Ask administrators how funding is used for language and literacy development, and discuss how it could be better used to support AAL speakers.** For example, Title 1 programs, such as the Every Student Succeeds Act (ESSA), often position AAL as problematic by using Standard English proficiency tests to identify AAL as a disorder (Boutte, Earick, & Jackson, 2021). This can result in AAL speakers being given Individualized Education Programs (IEPs) even though there is nothing wrong with their language. Likewise, Title III (Language Instruction for English Learners and Immigrant Students) monies are used to support English Language Learners but excludes AAL speakers.

Grandma Queen Palmer volunteering in the classroom

3. **Ask administrators to provide professional development on AAL and strategies for supporting AAL speakers.** Be sure those strategies allow them to maintain their first language (AAL) as they add Standard English to their repertoires.

4. **Find resources to learn more about AAL.** The two following examples are a good starting point. See the chart on the next page for more resources.

- **Kindergarten Through Grade 3: Four Things to Remember About African American Language: Examples From Children's Books.** *YC Young Children, 70*(4), 38–45. G. S. Boutte (2015).

- **Do educators see and honor biliteracy and bidialectalism in African American language speakers?** Apprehensions and reflections of two grandparents/professional educators. *Early Childhood Education Journal, 41*, 133–141. G. S. Boutte & G. L. Johnson (2013).

Revolutionary Love for Early Childhood Classrooms

Resources to Learn More About African American Language

- *Educating African American Students: And How Are the Children?* G. S. Boutte (Routledge, 2022)

- **Four Educational Considerations About African American Language (AAL): Examples from Children's Books.** *Young Children, 70*(4), 38–43. G. S. Boutte (2015)

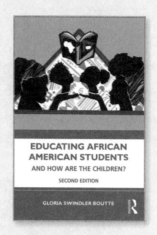

- **Do Educators See and Honor Biliteracy and Bidialectalism in African American Language Speakers?** Apprehensions and reflections of two grandparents/ professional educators. *Early Childhood Education Journal, 41*(2), 133–141. G. S. Boutte & G. Johnson (2013)

- *Funga Alafia:* Toward Welcoming, Understanding and Respecting African American Speakers' Bilingualism and Biliteracy. *Equity and Excellence in Education. Special Issue on Social Justice Approaches to African American Language and Literacies, 46*(3), 300–314. G. S. Boutte & G. L. Johnson (2013)

- *Revolutionary Love: Creating Culturally Inclusive Literacy Classrooms.* K. Wynter-Hoyte, E. Braden, M. Myers, S. C. Rodriguez, & N. Thornton (Scholastic, 2022)

- **YouTube: Talking Black in America: Do You Speak American?** (Parts 1, 2, and 3)

Chapter 5

CREATING CURRICULUM THAT CELEBRATES AFRICAN CULTURE AND LITERACIES

FIVE-YEAR-OLD TAMYKA CAN USUALLY BE FOUND "reading" one of the many books about African queens in her classroom's library. Her teacher, Ms. Collins, recently introduced Tamyka and her kindergarten classmates to a text set on African queens, which included books such as *Princess Akoto*, *Mufaro's Beautiful Daughters*, *Sense Pass King*, *African Kings and Queens*, and *African Princess*. Tamyka was fascinated to learn that Black women could be queens. To support Tamyka's (and other children's) interests, Ms. Collins posted photos of African queens throughout the classroom. She also put African kente cloth in the dress-up center so that children could immerse themselves in the theme of African kings and queens during dramatic play.

What Do Revolutionary Loving Teachers BELIEVE?

Revolutionary loving teachers believe that the curriculum should reflect and honor Black children's cultures and histories. For example, as revealed in the opening scenario, Ms. Collins believes it is important for all children to learn about Black history *before* enslavement. She has confidence that even young children can engage with information about African culture, past and present, when it is presented in accessible ways (Jackson et al., 2021).

Teachers who embrace revolutionary love believe that a variety of positive Black imagery should be displayed in classrooms all year long. They believe that Black children's hairstyles, clothing, and music preferences should be honored. They believe that children from other ethnic groups can learn about Black people and their culture and learn *from* them as well. Such is the case for teachers affiliated with the Center for the Education and Equity of African American Students (CEEAAS). All of their students learn about Black people around the globe, throughout history, beginning with Ancient Africa and spanning to contemporary times. This is essential to building African Diaspora Literacy, which is explained later in the chapter, and can be done in engaging ways, as proven by Ms. Collins, who put together the text set on African queens. Later in this chapter, we provide sample lessons and activities from CEEAAS teachers and other ECE educators. In their affirming, safe spaces, Black children are proud of their racial heritage and are engaged in instruction.

CEEAAS EC Teachers (clockwise from top left):
Ms. Janice Baines
Ms. Saudah Collins
Mrs. Jacqui Witherspoon
Ms. Mukkaramah Smith
Mr. Chris Hass
Ms. Mevelyn Gaither

Revolutionary loving teachers engage in deep, ongoing archaeological examinations of their own racial identities to understand how they mediate books and other resources that they share with children (Sealey-Ruiz, 2018). Guided by the belief that how they show up in classrooms is important, they understand the value of knowing themselves, including their preferences, biases, blind spots, and so on.

They reflect on how racial conversations are handled during instruction, particularly on how anti-Blackness (disdain for Black people and culture) reveals itself in classrooms via negative, stereotyping information in book collections, curriculum, instruction, assessment, and other aspects of schooling (Boutte & Bryan, 2019). Revolutionary loving teachers believe that because young children are developing their racial identities, it is important for educators to be intentional about exposing them to texts (e.g., books, media, and other sources) that represent a wide range of Black identities.

What Do Revolutionary Loving Teachers KNOW?

Revolutionary loving teachers know that Black children, like other children, are immersed in literacy activities in their homes and communities. Some activities may be "conventional," like reading and writing (see examples of toddler Carter below). Others may be culturally specific and include hand-clap games, church songs, contemporary music, overlapping conversations, and a wealth of other possibilities. Revolutionary loving teachers know that the process of learning about home literacies is both exciting and important. They also know how to connect home literacies to school literacies without privileging one over the other.

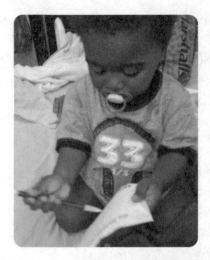
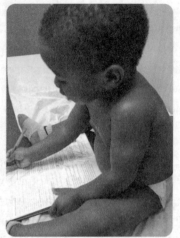
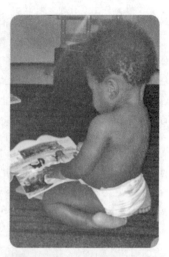
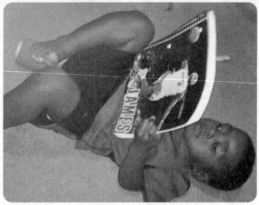

Toddler Carter engaged in literacies at home.

Revolutionary loving teachers *know* that an understanding of the cultures and histories of African descendant people is essential to the success of Black children. That understanding is commonly referred to as *African Diaspora Literacy (ADL)*. Educators who use ADL pedagogy recognize that Africa is the cradle of civilization and that they should look for the three core cultural continuities (see Chapter 2 for our highlight of *harmony, expression,* and *communication*) among Black children in their classrooms.

> ▶ What and when did you learn about African Diasporic people as a young child?
>
> ▶ Did you learn about kings and queens in Ancient Africa? How many can you name?
>
> ▶ How many countries are in Africa? How many African languages can you list here?

PAUSE & REFLECT

What Do Revolutionary Loving Teachers DO?

An African Diaspora Literacy instructional framework in the United States includes teaching about African people and their culture: 1) before enslavement, 2) during enslavement and afterward, and 3) in contemporary times (Boutte, 2016). Gloria recommends that coverage should include six major, overlapping historical periods:

1. **Ancient Africa (Ghana, Mali, Songhay, Ethiopia, Kush, etc.):** BCE (Before Common Era)–CE (Common Era)

2. **Enslavement: 1619–1865** (We acknowledge the presence of Africans in the Americas before 1619, but use this date to align with school curricula)

3. **Reconstruction: 1865–1877**

4. **Jim Crow: 1890–1965/1970**

5. **Black Nationalist/Civil Rights: 1954–1968**

6. **Contemporary (U.S. and Diaspora): 1969–present**

Though these six periods are presented sequentially here, there is a lot of overlap so they don't need to be presented in a linear fashion. As children (and teachers) become literate about the African Diaspora, an emphasis on African American cultural dimensions and Black people's agency, joy, and resistance (based on small and large examples) will be important generative themes that are revisited. African Diasporic content should be interdisciplinary and include interdisciplinary content from literacy, history, art, music, science, and other subjects (Boutte, 2021).

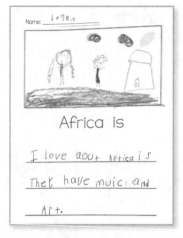

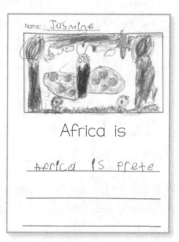

(Above) First graders reflect on their lessons about Africa.

(Below) Mrs. Collins' classroom decor

Any study of African people should begin with relevant history that predates contact with Europeans. This is important for demonstrating that African descendant people, like all humans, are not acultural (Boutte, 2022). For example, when Africans were brought to the United States by force and enslaved, they brought with them rich cultural legacies, which have changed over time, while also sustaining deep cultural aspects such as the values of harmony, expression, and communication, as described in Chapter 2. Gloria (2021) emphasizes four principles of African Diaspora Literacy for early childhood settings.

Principles of African Diaspora Literacy

PRINCIPLE 1: African Diaspora Literacy can and should be used with young children.

Elsewhere we have addressed a young child's ability to make sense of concepts beyond the here and now (Boutte & Strickland, 2008). For example, young children readily include dinosaurs, fairy tales, unicorns, and other concepts in their cognitive repertoires. Importantly, as young children are developing their foundational racial identities, they need to interact with African people's perspectives as foundational in a racialized world. The omission of African perspectives sends the message that African ancestry is not important, nonexistent, and not worth studying (Boutte, 2021). The ongoing use of African Diasporic literature interrupts these faulty narratives.

Looking for African Diaspora Literature?

Search the Scholastic Teacher Store online for collections related to Black children as well as the Mahogany Books website for lists of relevant children's books.

Visit Sankofa's YouTube page for read-aloud videos.

PRINCIPLE 2: African Diaspora Literature collections should be comprehensive, iterative, and generative.

Collections (e.g., books, art, music, media, videos, websites) and resources should be layered across disciplines and modes. They should also be comprehensive in terms of 1) gender (e.g., male/female/transgender/nonbinary); 2) geographic regions throughout the diaspora (e.g., rural, urban, suburban); 3) religions; 4) ages; 5) abilities; and other social identities. The goal is to teach about Black brilliance, joy, agency, and resistance across disciplines, historical periods, locales, and people. Remember to always start by focusing on the children in your classrooms and/or make connections to their lives and ways of knowing. Teach about community sages (e.g., local elders and leaders in Black communities) and invite them into your setting regularly as part of your community.

PRINCIPLE 3: African Diaspora Literacy is important for White children and children of color.

Rudine Sims Bishop (1990) used the metaphors of *mirrors* and *windows* to convey the importance of including representation/reflections of all children in books (mirrors), as well as of cultures and worlds beyond their own (windows). As we've recommended in previous chapters, providing mirrors (affirmations) for children of African ancestry is critically important for the development of positive racial identities. Likewise, other children benefit from learning *about* and *from* African diasporic people and perspectives (Boutte 2022). ADL book collections provide not only mirrors but also windows for Black children as they are being exposed to other stories and experiences. Many book collections provide far too many reflections of whiteness, and far too few of people of color, and those that are provided often contain inaccurate or distorted representations.

PRINCIPLE 4: Children's literature is not sufficient to counter the omissions of and inaccuracies about Black people globally.

Without a doubt, high-quality, culturally relevant children's literature is essential for developing positive racial identities for Black children. We emphasize that the literature should be critically examined by teachers for its authenticity regarding the storylines, illustrations, and messages. They should be pro-Black, which means the focus should be on positive, Black racial identities. We suggest using literature that emphasizes larger themes about Black culture mentioned in Chapter 1 (e.g., communalism, perseverance). These should be revisited often across disciplines. Importantly, children's literature should be layered across other media including songs, everyday experiences, videos, and so forth.

Using the Black cultural theme of *communication*, we present a layered text set to illuminate its existence and manifestation across time. Using this approach allows for deepening Black children's understandings and development of their racial identities. It also teaches other children about the beauty, joy, and agency of Black culture across time. We note that text sets can address more than one Black cultural dimension. We focus on one dimension, *communication* (which includes *affect, communalism,* and *social time perspective*), to emphasize cultural continuity in Black culture across time.

Often, we use Adinkra symbols to graphically depict African Diasporic values. Adinkra symbols originated from the Akan people of Côte d'Ivoire and Ghana, and represent values, principles, proverbs, philosophies, thoughts,

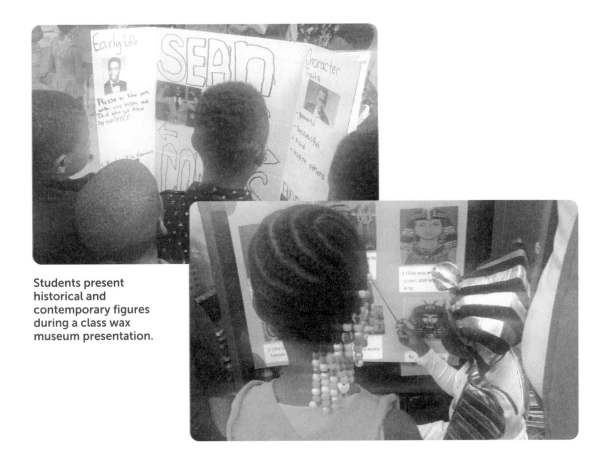

Students present historical and contemporary figures during a class wax museum presentation.

and wisdom (Owusu, 2019). Values and principles such as democracy, courage, perseverance, wisdom, and freedom are conveyed via beautiful symbolism. The foundational African values conveyed by Adinkra symbols are robust and intergenerational. While recognizing the huge variation among and within the 55 African countries—comprising more than 3,000 ethnic groups and 1,500+ languages—we use Adinkra symbols as a proxy for African cultures. That is, while the Adinkra symbols are West African, the principles and lessons they represent reflect Black cultural legacies around the globe (Boutte, 2016).

Two common Adinkra symbols that represent communalism (a style of Communication) can be seen below: Nkonsonkonson and Funtunfunefu-Denkyemfunefu. These visuals can be used to reinforce the larger theme of communalism.

The chart on the following pages lists texts that represent critically conscious choices that can help deepen children's understandings.

Adinkra Symbols Representing the Three Core Practices

Adinkra Symbol	Meaning
	NKONSONKONSON Unity and human relations
	FUNTUNFUNEFU-DENKYEMFUNEFU "Siamese crocodiles." Two crocodiles sharing one stomach A symbol of democracy and unity

Sample Texts That Focus on Communication Among African Descendant People Across Time

Summary of Text	Commentary About Communication	Possible Multimodal Layers*
Historical Period: Ancient Africa		
Our People (Medearis, 1994) *Our People* shares a conversation between a father and daughter as he teaches her the history of Black people from Ancient Africa to the present day.	This book provides an intergenerational perspective of Black people's collective accomplishments over time.	• MUSIC VIDEO: "I Can"—Nas (may be more appropriate for 2nd and 3rd graders) • VIDEO READ-ALOUD: *Storytime: Our People* • VIDEO: Ancient Egypt for Kids (Kids Black History) • VIDEO: How to Make Paper Pyramids (very easy) • WEBSITE: Kente Cloth and Styles • WEBSITE: Hieroglyphic Alphabet
Sense Pass King: A Story From Cameroon (Tchana, 2002) This enchanting folktale is set in ancient Cameroon. It features a young girl who is born to be a leader and who focuses on the welfare of the people in seven villages.	Despite the King's efforts to keep the main character from living her purpose of being a queen, she uses her wisdom to respect everyone so that the kingdom prospers.	• VIDEO READ-ALOUD: *Sense Pass King* • VIDEO: An Amazing Djembe Solo by Master Djembe Drummer: M'Bemba Bangoura
African Princess: The Amazing Lives of Africa's Royal Women (Hansen, 2004) This book describes the lives of six queens and princesses.	This book shows how African women governed and protected their kingdoms and focused on the welfare of their respective community members.	• VIDEO READ-ALOUD: *Mufaro's Beautiful Daughters* • VIDEO: Top 10 African Queens You Need to Know About.

*Please do an Internet search for suggested videos and music listed in this chart.

Summary of Text	Commentary About Communication	Possible Multimodal Layers*
Historical Period: Enslavement		
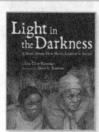 ***Light in the Darkness: A Story About How Slaves Learned in Secret*** (Cline-Ransome, 2013) This story is about a young girl and her mother learning to read in a hidden school during enslavement.	This book shows the communal value of literacy among African descendant people who were enslaved. It illuminates communal organization during treacherous times in the face of violent outcomes for learning to read.	• VIDEO READ-ALOUD: *Light in the Darkness* • VIDEO: "Wade in the Water"—Sweet Honey in the Rock • VIDEO READ-ALOUD: *The 1619 Project: Born on the Water* • SONG: "Stand Up"—Cynthia Erivo
 ***Moses: When Harriet Tubman Led Her People to Freedom*** (Weatherford, 2006) In lyrical text, this book shows how Harriet Tubman drew on her faith to guide many people to freedom.	This book explains how Harriet Tubman's bravery led her to return 19 times to the South to free others.	• VIDEO: The Breathtaking Courage of Harriet Tubman—Janell Hobson • VIDEO: Harriet Tubman Story • VIDEO READ-ALOUD: *Follow the Drinking Gourd* • VIDEO: "Lift Ev'ry Voice and Sing" (Black national anthem) • VIDEO READ-ALOUD: *Henry's Freedom Box*
 ***Freedom Soup*** (Charles, 2021) A Haitian grandmother shares a holiday, a family recipe, and a story of freedom with her granddaughter.	*Freedom Soup* shows how Haitian people organized and ejected the British from their country.	• VIDEO READ-ALOUD: *Freedom Soup* • Lauture, D. (2021). *The epic story of Toussaint Louverture*. Thorobred Books.

*Please do an Internet search for suggested videos and music listed in this chart.

Summary of Text	Commentary About Communication	Possible Multimodal Layers*
Historical Period: Reconstruction		
 ***Ellen's Broom*** (Lyons, 2012) Set during Reconstruction, this story shares the pride that a young girl has when her parents are able to "legally" marry, while also maintaining the African and African American tradition of jumping the broom.	This book tells the story of many people who were enslaved who wanted to marry legally but were not allowed to. Nevertheless, their love persevered. The book emphasizes the value and centrality of Black families during and after enslavement.	• VIDEO READ-ALOUD: *Ellen's Broom* • VIDEO: The Incredible Story of Robert Smalls
Historical Period: Jim Crow		
 ***Going Down Home with Daddy*** (Lyons, 2019) A Black family travels to the South for a family reunion.	This book lovingly shows a celebration of Black history, culture, and the power of family traditions.	• VIDEO READ-ALOUD: *Going Down Home with Daddy* • SONG: "We Are Family"—Sister Sledge
 ***White Socks Only*** (Coleman, 1996) A little girl in Mississippi tries to drink from a "Whites Only" water fountain and is shoved by a White man. The community comes to her rescue.	This beautiful story shows how the Black community worked together to protect children during the Jim Crow era.	• SONG: "Glory"—Common, John Legend • SONG: "Ain't Gonna Let Nobody Turn Me Around"—Jurnee Smollett

*Please do an Internet search for suggested videos and music listed in this chart.

Summary of Text	Commentary About Communication	Possible Multimodal Layers*
Historical Period: Jim Crow *continued*		
 ***Ruth and the Green Book*** (Ramsey, 2010) A Black family drives from Chicago to Alabama at a time when it was difficult for Black Americans to travel in certain parts of the country.	The organization of Black people led to the development of a guidebook listing places that would welcome Black visitors so that they could travel safely.	• VIDEO READ-ALOUD: *Ruth and the Green Book*
 ***New Shoes*** (Myers, 2015) Set in the Jim Crow era, a young girl learns how to stand up against the racial discrimination she faced when shopping for new shoes.	This book illustrates how Black people often created businesses during the Jim Crow era rather than give money to discriminatory White businesses.	• VIDEO READ-ALOUD: *New Shoes*
 ***The Great Migration: An American Story*** (Lawrence, 1995) The paintings of Jacob Lawrence are used to tell the story about African Americans who moved for a better life.	This book captures the spirit of the more than six million Black people who had the courage and agency to try to build better lives for themselves in the North.	• VIDEO: *Harlem Renaissance* (Flocabulary)

*Please do an Internet search for suggested videos and music listed in this chart.

Revolutionary Love for Early Childhood Classrooms

Summary of Text	Commentary About Communication	Possible Multimodal Layers*
Historical Period: Civil Rights/Black Nationalism		
 *Sit-in: How Four Friends Stood Up by Sitting Down* (Pinkney, 2010) This book celebrates the Woolworth's lunch counter sit-in in Greensboro, North Carolina, when four college students staged a peaceful protest that became a defining moment in the struggle for racial equality and the growing civil rights movement.	Here is a story of the collective organization and tenacity of Black college students across the nation who participated in sit-ins and demonstrations to demand equal treatment.	• SONG: "Something Inside So Strong"—AIC Freedom School Finale • SONG: "We Shall Overcome"—Louis Armstrong (with lyrics)
 *Freedom on the Menu: The Greensboro Sit-ins* (Weatherford, 2005) Set in North Carolina, a young girl yearns for equal rights and discovers things that Black people could do to address unfair policies and laws.	This story illuminates how Black people organized sit-ins to fight for their freedom and rights.	• MUSIC VIDEO: "Freedom"—Beyoncé (featuring Kendrick Lamar) • SONG: "A Change Is Gonna Come"—Sam Cooke

*Please do an Internet search for suggested videos and music listed in this chart.

Summary of Text	Commentary About Communication	Possible Multimodal Layers*
Historical Period: Contemporary Life in African Diaspora		
 ***Our Children Can Soar: A Celebration of Rosa, Barack, and the Pioneers of Change*** (Cook, 2009) This is a presentation of the intergenerational achievements of Black people.	Learn how each generation benefits from achievements of previous generations and Black people's collective contributions.	• SONG: "Rise Up"—Cardinal Shehan School Choir for the Ravens
 ***Ogbo: Sharing Life in an African Village*** (Onyefulu, 1996) A young girl shares examples of Nigerian culture in contemporary society.	This book describes how each age group in a family-like community has specific roles.	• SONG: "In My Africa" (from TV series *Arthur*) • SONG: "Every Ghetto, Every City"—Lauryn Hill
 ***Ikenna Goes to Nigeria*** (Onyefulu, 2007) This contemporary story highlights connections between a Nigerian-English boy and his Nigerian roots.	Communalism is evident in the family's insistence to maintain ties between relatives in England and relatives in Nigeria. Cultural continuity is important.	• Children dance to Afrobeats music.

*Please do an Internet search for suggested videos and music listed in this chart.

Text sets can be used as a part of an inquiry unit that spans several weeks. As teachers engage in ADL pedagogy, we suggest ongoing use of African drumming, Black music, and songs in early childhood classrooms. Introduction to African American Language should also be a key component. Teachers are encouraged to make intergenerational connections across the text sets when possible. For example, if discussing enslavement, teachers may emphasize skills and wisdom from Ancient Africa that Black people used. Likewise, teachers can point out how similar skills and wisdom are still used today or have been used across historical eras.

What Can You DO NOW in the Classroom?

1. **Take a moment to reflect on the literacies (e.g., books, songs, languages) that are represented and accepted in your classroom, school, or center.** Write a list of what is missing in terms of Black culture and action steps to fill this void.

2. **Look at the suggested/required packing guides, thematic units, etc.** In what ways is Black culture represented? Take a moment to critically analyze your classroom curriculum. Pay attention to the books that are suggested/required in pacing guides, thematic units, etc. Do the picture books feature more animals than Black children? Do the picture books feature more White characters than children of color? For the picture books that include Black characters, are they tokenized, marginalized, and/or stereotyped? Meir Muller (2021) recommends the following sample questions and prompts to help educators analyze the books in their collections and move toward critically conscious Black book collections and resources:

   - Are Black people included in this text? Why or why not?

   - Do you see anything unfair to Black people? Tell me more about this.

   - Who or what is shown as necessary? How was the message of importance conveyed?

   - Are Black people left out or shown as unimportant? How was this message conveyed?

- Can this message be hurtful or unfair to Black people? Why?

- How does the text make you feel? Why?

- What can you do to improve this issue?

What Can You DO IN THE UPCOMING WEEKS?

1. **After you have examined the curriculum, take some time to build your classroom library and materials.** Do not feel obligated to spend money on these materials. Instead, visit your local library, use the websites that we mentioned throughout, and start a wish list for your classroom.

2. **A simple way to ensure symbolic and curricular affirmations of Black culture in ECE classrooms is a week-long study of names near the beginning of the school year.** You may start with daily read-alouds from a text set of books that honor names from different cultures (see below). In this case, it should be emphasized that all names are respected, and you may want to help children learn about their own names.

Sample text set on names

3. **Have students start a "Where I Am From" shoe box.** Students can collect items in their homes and communities that represent them. These items can be used for writing instruction, art activities, etc.

4. **Create class books to add to your library.** By personalizing the books, you can help students make connections with their own lives, and spark interest in these books.

Ms. Collins, mentioned at the beginning of the chapter, works with ECE children to develop a class book with a page for each child. For her first-grade class, Ms. Collins used predictable text on each page (*School is in! Look, here is our friend, [insert child's name]*). This book and other personalized, teacher-made books are often children's favorite books.

Sample pages from teacher-made class book of names featuring children

Kamania includes name stories with her preservice teachers each semester in her reading methods course. This is a great tool for educators and students to get to know each other and connect with families to research the story of their names.

Sample pages from teacher-made class book of names featuring children

Asar Jaleel McLawhorn

Asar is my name.
No Asar is the same.
Read along to find out
What my name is all about.
Asar es mi nombre
No hay otra Asar igual.
Lee para aprender
Más sobre mi nombre.

Asar is an ancient East African name. It has an importance in many faiths and resonates with "the way of life." It was given by my mom with the idea of merging oneself with love regardless of challenges.

My name story
Has come to an end
Keep on reading
And meet my new friend!

La historia de mi nombre
Ha llegado a su fin.
Seguir leyendo
Y para conocer a mi nuevo amigo.

Gloria helped her grandchildren understand that in the cultures of African descendant people, names have meanings. She shared the concept of "day names" used by the Akan people in Ghana, West Africa. The Akan people believe that everyone is born with a purpose and the day that we are born is related to that purpose. With this activity, students can research their day name if they wish. This example was completed by Gloria's grandson, Carter, when he was eight years old. She and Carter discussed the meanings of his first, middle, and last names as well as the origins. Gloria asked Carter what he thought about his name. Activities like this can be ongoing and allow children to think about the meanings of their names often.

Of course, children's names should not be abbreviated without their permission or joked about. Classmates should be encouraged to use the child's *preferred* names.

Name Study

	Name	Meaning	Origin	Thoughts About Name
First Name	Carter	One who transports goods by boats	Irish English Scottish	I love it!
Middle Name	Nathaniel	God has given	Greek form of Hebrew	I like it
Last Name	Archie	Truly brave	German	Love the meaning
Day Name	Rafi			

Gloria created a Name Study template for Carter to fill out.

What Can You DO BEYOND YOUR CLASSROOM?

1. **There is a wealth of knowledge in Black communities that is rooted in African cultural dimensions.** Think about how you can tap into that knowledge and invite community members into your classroom. For example, we recently saw a school district on social media that invites renowned local Black children's book authors to visit schools in their community. These authors highlight African cultural dimensions in their work and embody them during their visits.

2. **Other community visits can include Black business owners.** Invite Black people from different countries to visit your class and share their stories.

3. **Find ways for students to connect digitally with other students across the African Diaspora.** Have students blog/email/video chat with other students.

4. **Take a local field trip to a Black community where students can compare and contrast cultural and linguistic practices with the African Diaspora.** Use these field trips as opportunities to elaborate about our travels and the commonalities we see.

In Closing

We hope that you have gained a deeper love for Black children and their brilliance. Please use this book as a catapult and a reference to return to when honoring Black culture in your spaces. We thank you for the work that you are doing and know the strategies provided will move you toward a revolutionary love for the children you teach and communities you serve.

We will end this book with the same three words we used to open:
We love you!

APPENDIX A

Features of African American Language

Phonological Features of AAL and SE		
FEATURES/RULES	**AAL**	**SE**
Substitution of the "th" phoneme (sound)	dem wif, wit, or wid	them with
Different stress patterns	po'lice	po lice'
No distinction between words that sound alike	fine/find = fine cold/coal = coal mask/mass = mass	fine/fine cold/coal mask/mass
Consonant blends are often substituted or deleted (consonant cluster reduction or non production)	axe	ask

Examples of AAL Syntax		
FEATURES/RULES	**AAL**	**SE**
Make it simple—e.g., delete linking verbs.	You a pretty girl.	You are a pretty girl.
Two or more negatives are allowed.	You don't have no shoes.	You don't have any shoes.
Use of the habitual "be" to connote perpetual emphases	He be hittin me.	He is always hitting me. *Note: There is no direct literal SE interpretation for the habitual* be

Examples of AAL Syntax		
FEATURES/RULES	**AAL**	**SE**
Regularize when possible—maintain same form	I is We is You is You is He, She, or It is They is *Note: The verb remains the same throughout (regularization)*	I am We are You are You are He, She, or It is They are *Note: The verb changes— is irregular*
Regularize when possible—maintain same form **Third-Person Singular remains the same**	I swim We swim You swim You swim He, She, or It swim They swim	I swim We swim You swim You swim He, She, or It swims They swim *Note: The verb change in third-person singular*
Regularize when possible—maintain same form **Reflective Pronouns do not change form**	His/Hisself Their/Theirselves	His/Himself Their/Themselves
Plurals	five cent *Note: The plural marker is the number itself (more than one = plural)*	five cents *Note: There are two plural markers: The number "five" and the "s" on "cents"*
Possessive	John chair Baby mama *Note: The possessor (John) serves to indicate possession*	John's chair Baby's mama *Note: There are two possessive markers: the name of the possessor "John" and the apostrophe "s"*

Examples of AAL Syntax

FEATURES/RULES	AAL	SE
Past tense	I look out the window. *Note: Typically will not hear or see the "ed" in writing or orally. However, sometimes the "ed" is overemphasized (hypercorrection) and the oral pronunciation becomes "look-D" (Smitherman, 1977/1985)*	I looked out the window.
Topicalization	That teacher she mean. (two topics/subjects— "teacher" and "she")	The teacher is mean.

Examples of Semantics

FEATURES/RULES	AAL	SE
Keep the language generative; improvise; be creative.	"shawty" (shorty)—a female; someone that a person likes "swag"—style	Slang is used, but not typically generated; often co-opted from AAL; do not change as rapidly as AAL
Use cultural inversion—reverse the meaning and function of words.	"dawg" (dog)—term of endearment	Not typically done
Speak in codes.	Symbolism— Metaphors; coded language in songs, quilts, folktales, etc.	Symbolism exists, but is often used formally in books, speeches, music— not necessarily in everyday speech

Examples of Pragmatics

FEATURES/RULES	AAL	SE
Communicate impressively.	Signifying; Playing with the Language	
Speak with soul, personal style, and verve.	Circular and energetic conversations are okay. Dramatic repetition is used. Episodic stories	Mundane/lackluster—even-toned, occasional changes in tone Topic-centered stories
More than one person can speak at a time.	Overlapping and co-narration is permitted.	Sequential; turn-taking
Speak directly. Be efficient.	Direct commands	Indirect commands
Use nonverbal language.		
Involve your audience.	Call and response	Okay to talk to a group without involvement from the group

Source: Boutte, G. S. (2007). Teaching African American English speakers: Expanding educators and student repertoires. In M. E. Brisk, (Ed.). *Language, culture, and community in teacher education*, pp. 47–70. Routledge.

APPENDIX B

11 Dimensions of African American Culture in Practice

How to Apply the Dimensions	Activity Ideas
1 Spirituality	
• Make the meaning and purpose of activities and lessons clear to children. • Involve multisensory and multidimensional aspects to teaching (e.g., not worksheets alone). • Show connections between the past and the present. • Help students reflect on their life's purpose (why they exist), gifts, interests, and goals.	• Yoga for children • Deep breathing and calming exercises • Reading affirmations Read aloud: • (Age 5) *The Day You Begin* by Jacqueline Woodson • (Ages 6–8) *Anansi the Spider: A Tale From the Ashanti* by Gerald McDermott
2 Harmony	
• Teach about Africans and African Americans who work(ed) in concert with nature (e.g., George Washington Carver; farmers; midwives; doctors using natural remedies). • Research African American naturalists, such as South Carolinian topiary artist Pearl Fryar and ornithologist J. Drew Lanham. • Help students connect to nature by involving them in outside adventures and excursions.	• Yoga for children • Deep breathing and calming exercises • Observational walks Read aloud: • (Age 5) *I Am Enough* by Grace Byers • (Ages 6–8) Biographies about Black people from all six historical periods • (Ages 6–8) *African Folk Tales* by Hugh Vernon-Jackson

How to Apply the Dimensions	Activity Ideas
3 **Movement**	
• Engage children often in movement, rhythm, percussiveness, music, and dance.	• African and African American dance • Culturally appropriate role-play • Handplays • Black music from many genres (e.g., *Shake It to the One That You Love the Best*—book with lyrics and music CD) Read aloud: • (Age 5) *Max Found Two Sticks* by Brian Pinkney • (Ages 6–8) *Swing Sisters: The Story of the International Sweethearts of Rhythm* by Karen Deans
4 **Verve**	
• Allow for creativity in assignments (e.g., creative writing, spoken word, musical/dance interpretations).	• Handclapping chants (see YouTube video Sesame Street: Handclapping Chants) • Hip hop pedagogy (visit the *Flocabulary* website for educational hip hop videos and activities)
5 **Affect**	
• Engage the humanities for assignments.	• Dramatic play and role-play • Create videos • Analyze the meaning of freedom songs Read aloud: • (Age 5) *Brown Boy Joy* by Thomishia Booker • (Ages 6–8) *Momma, Did You Hear the News?* by Sanya Whittaker Gragg

How to Apply the Dimensions	Activity Ideas
6 Communalism	
• Emphasize the South African principle *Ubuntu* (I am because we are). • Integrate information about Black communities and sages and living history (e.g., regularly bring in elders, sages, from community). • Balance individual and group learning. • Support peer tutoring and offer scaffolding.	Read aloud: • (Age 5) *Our Children Can Soar: A Celebration of Rosa, Barack, and the Pioneers of Change* by Michelle Cook • (Ages 6–8) *Going Down Home With Daddy* by Kelly Starling Lyons
7 Expressive Individualism	
• Observe examples of the unique ways that African American students express themselves while also reflecting Black culture (e.g., a student who wears multiple African bracelets on her wrist; hairstyles). • Engage children in culturally relevant math/science and ethnomathematics/ ethnoscience where they can see the cultural influence on math and science.	• Multiple means of expression (e.g., videos, songs, collages, written papers, spoken word) • Develop class books around a theme in which children can show their take on the theme. Read aloud: • (Ages 6–8) *Crown: An Ode to the Fresh Cut* by Derrick Barnes
8 Oral tradition	
• Integrate oral traditions like songs into routine activities such as attendance. • Feature and invite orators from Black communities. • Teach about well-known orators and performers (e.g., Malcolm X, Sojourner Truth, Martin Luther King, Septima Clark, Modjeska Simkins, Maya Angelou). • Teach about literacy in African kingdoms before enslavement.	• Tap into Black students' legacy of oral tradition: debate teams, oral reports, and drumming (e.g., talking drums). Read aloud: • (Age 5) *Hey Black Child* by Useni Eugene Perkins • (Ages 6–8) *Flossie and the Fox* by Patricia McKissack • (Ages 6–8) Br'er Rabbit folktales

How to Apply the Dimensions	Activity Ideas
9 **Social Time Perspective**	
• Teach how indigenous people read signs from nature (e.g., moss, stars, blooms). • Value people and relationships (e.g., talking with others is not wasting time).	Read aloud: • (Age 5) *So Much!* by Trish Cooke • (Ages 6–8) *Follow the Drinking Gourd* by Jeanette Winter
10 **Perseverance**	
• Remind students of ancestors, family members, and community members who persisted, despite hardships. • Focus on the legacy of resistance, rebellions, and agency among Black people and communities. • Teach about the history of Mother Emanuel Church in Charleston, SC, and other thriving Black towns in the 1800s and 1900s. • Share narratives and biographies (written and other media forms) of African descendant people who were enslaved.	Read aloud: • (Age 5) *Ruby Bridges Goes to School: My True Story* by Ruby Bridges • (Ages 6–8) *The Story of Ruby Bridges* by Robert Coles
11 **Improvisation**	
• Teach about historical improvisations used by Black people (e.g., Denmark Vesey's rebellion; learning to read). • Focus on how improvisation is used in the humanities (e.g., jazz, blues, cooking, language, quilting).	• Allow for improvisation during activities Read aloud: • (Ages 6–8) *Light in the Darkness: A Story About How Slaves Learned in Secret* by Lesa Cline-Ransome

Sources: Adapted with permission from: Boutte (2022).

APPENDIX C

Adinkra Symbols

Symbol	Name	Meaning
	Gye Nyame	A symbol that represents great power
	Sankofa	A symbol that represents wisdom in learning from the past. I learn from my past.
	Adinkrahene	A symbol of authority, leadership, and charisma
	Dwennimmen	A symbol of wisdom and learning

Adinkra Symbol Cut-Outs

Gye Nyame
I am protected by great power.

Sankofa
I learn from my past.

Adinkrahene
I am a good leader.

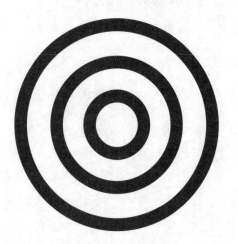

Dwennimmen
I am wise.

CHILDREN'S BOOKS CITED

Amadi, P., & Amadi, N. (2019). *Chichi and Didi love their names*. Independently Published.

Barnes, D. (2017). *Crown: An ode to the fresh cut*. Agate Bolden.

Booker, T. (2018). *Brown boy joy*. Hey Carter Children's Book Series.

Bridges, R. (2016). *Ruby Bridges goes to school: My true story*. Scholastic.

Byers, G. (2018). *I am enough*. Balzer & Bray.

Charles, T. (2021). *Freedom soup*. Candlewick.

Choi, Y. (2003). *The name jar*. Dragonfly Books.

Cline-Ransome, L. (2013). *Light in the darkness: A story about how slaves learned in secret*. Little, Brown Books for Young Readers.

Coleman, E. (1996). *White socks only*. Albert Whitman & Company.

Coles, R. (1995). *The story of Ruby Bridges*. Scholastic.

Cook, M. (2012). *Our children can soar: A celebration of Rosa, Barack, and the pioneers of change*. Bloomsbury USA Childrens.

Cooke, T. (2008). *So Much!* Candlewick.

Coombs, K. (2021). *Little naturalists: George Washington Carver loved plants*. Babylit.

Coombs, K. (2021). *Little Naturalists: Wangari Maathai planted trees*. Babylit.

Deans, K. (2015). *Swing sisters: The story of the international sweethearts of rhythm*. Holiday House.

Duncan, A. F. (1995). *Willie Jerome*. Atheneum.

Duncan, A. F. (2005). *Honey baby sugar child*. Simon & Schuster Books for Young Readers.

Gragg, S. W. (2017). *Momma, did you hear the news?* CreateSpace Independent Publishing Platform.

Hansen, J. (2004). *African Princess: The amazing lives of Africa's royal women*. Jump at the Sun.

Hesse, K. (1999). *Come On, Rain!* Scholastic.

Lawrence, J. (1995). *The Great Migration: An American story*. HarperCollins.

Levine, E. (2007). *Henry's Freedom Box: A True Story from the Underground Railroad*. Scholastic.

Lyons, K. S. (2012). *Ellen's broom*. GP Putnam's Sons Books for Young Readers.

Lyons, K. S. (2019). *Going down home with daddy*. Peachtree.

McDermott, G. (1987). *Anansi the spider: A tale from the Ashanti*. Henry Holt & Company.

McKissack, P. C. (1986). *Flossie and the fox*. Dial Books.

Medearis, A. S. (1994). *Our people*. Gingham Dog Press.

Mendez, P. (1989). *The Black snowman*. Scholastic.

Myers, S. L. (2015). *New shoes*. Holiday House.

Ofori, I. E., & Ofori, B. (2020). *Princess Akoto: The story of the golden stool and the Ashanti Kingdom*. Tellwell Talent.

Onyefulu, I. (1996). *Ogbo: Sharing life in an African village*. Gulliver Books.

Onyefulu, I. (2000). *Ebele's favourite: A book of African games*. Frances Lincoln Children's Books.

Onyefulu, I. (2007). *Ikenna goes to Nigeria*. Frances Lincoln Children's Books.

Onyefulu, I. (2011). *Omer's favorite place*. Frances Lincoln Children's Books.

Onyefulu, I. (2013). *Look at this! Play*. Frances Lincoln Children's Books.

Perkins, U. E. (2019). *Hey Black child*. LB Kids.

Pinkney, A. D. (2020). *Sit-in: How four friends stood up by sitting down*. Little, Brown Books for Young Readers.

Pinkney, B. (1997). *Max found two sticks*. Aladdin Paperbacks.

Ramsey, C. A. (2010). *Ruth and the green book*. Carolrhoda Books.

Raschka, C. (2007). *Yo! Yes?* Scholastic.

Recorvits, H. (2014). *My name is Yoon*. Square Fish.

Ringgold, F. (1996). *Tar beach*. Dragonfly Books.

Robinson, A. (2020). *The modern day black alphabet*. lyn-111.

Rochelle, B. (1994). *When Jo Louis won the title*. Houghton Mifflin Harcourt.

Rosales, M. B. (1996). *'Twas the night b'fore Christmas*. Cartwheel Books.

Schofield-Morrison, C. (2014). *I got the rhythm*. Bloomsbury USA Childrens.

Smalls, I. (2004). *Don't say ain't*. Charlesbridge.

Steptoe, J. (2018). *Mufaro's beautiful daughters*. Lothrop Lee & Shepard.

Tarpley, N. A. (2001). *I love my hair!* Little, Brown Books for Young Readers.

Tarpley, N. A. (2009). *Bibbity bop barbershop*. Little, Brown Books for Young Readers.

Tchana, K. H. (2002). *Sense Pass King: A story from Cameroon*. Holiday House.

Thompkins-Bigelow, J. (2020). *Your name is a song*. The Innovation Press.

Vernon-Jackson, H. (1999). *African folk tales*. Dover Publications.

Weatherford, C. B. (2005). *Freedom on the menu: The Greensboro sit-ins*. Puffin Books.

Weatherford, C. B. (2006). *Moses: When Harriet Tubman led her people to freedom*. Hyperion Books.

Williams, K., & Mohammed, K. (2009). *My name is Sangoel*. Eerdmans Books for Young Readers.

Williams, S. A. (1997). *Working cotton*. Clarion Books.

Winter, J. (1992). *Follow the drinking gourd*. Dragonfly Books.

Woodson, J. (2018). *The day you begin*. Nancy Paulsen Books.

Woodson, J. (2022). *The year we learned to fly*. Nancy Paulsen Books.

REFERENCES

Aboud, F. E. (2008). A social-cognitive developmental theory of prejudice. *Handbook of Race, Racism, and the Developing Child*, 55–71.

Alim, H. S., & Smitherman, G. (2012). *Articulate while black: Barack Obama, language, and race in the U.S.* Oxford University Press.

Baugh, J. (1999). *Out of the mouths of slaves: African American language and educational malpractice.* University of Texas Press.

Bishop, R. S. (1990). Mirrors, windows and sliding glass doors. *Perspectives, 6*(3), ix-xi.

Boutte, G. S. (1992). Frustrations of an African-American parent: A personal and professional account. *The Phi Delta Kappan, 73*(10), 786-788.

Boutte, G. S. (2007). Teaching African American English speakers: Expanding educators and student repertoires. In M. E. Brisk (Ed.). *Language, culture, and community in teacher education* (pp. 47–70). Routledge.

Boutte, G. S. (2015). Kindergarten Through Grade 3: Four Things to Remember About African American Language: Examples From Children's Books. *Young Children, 70*(4), 38–45.

Boutte, G. S. (2016). *Educating African-American students: And how are the children?* Routledge.

Boutte, G. S. (2021). African Diasporic literature book collections for young children. In H. Adams (Ed.), *Transforming practice. Transforming lives through diverse children's literature*, pp. 101–110. Primary English Teaching Association Australia (PETAA).

Boutte, G. S. (2022). *Educating African American students: And how are the children? (2nd ed.).* Routledge.

Boutte, G., & Bryan, N. (2021). When will Black children be well? Interrupting anti-Black violence in early childhood classrooms and schools. *Contemporary Issues in Early Childhood, 22*(3), 232–243.

Boutte, G. S., & Compton-Lilly, C. (2022). Prioritizing Pro-Blackness in literacy research, scholarship, and teaching. *Journal of Early Childhood Literacy, 22*(3), 323–334.

Boutte, G. S., & DeFlorimonte, D. (1998). The complexities of valuing cultural differences without overemphasizing them: Taking it to the next level. *Equity & Excellence, 31*(3), 58–62.

Boutte, G. S., & Johnson, G. (2012). Do educators see and honor biliteracy and bidialectalism in African American Language speakers? Apprehensions and reflections of two grandparents/professional educators. *Early Childhood Education Journal, 41*(2), 133–141.

Boutte, G. S., & Johnson, G. L., Jr. (2013). *Funga Alafia.* Toward welcoming, understanding and respecting African American Speakers' bilingualism and biliteracy. *Equity and Excellence in Education. Special Issue on Social Justice Approaches to African American Language and Literacies, 46*(3), 300–314.

Boutte, G. S., Jackson, T. O., & Earick, M. E. (2021). Linguistic policies for African American Language speakers: Moving from anti-Blackness to pro-Blackness. *Theory Into Practice.*

Boutte, G. S., King, J. E., Johnson, G. L., & King, L. J. (Eds.). (2021). *We be lovin' Black children: Learning to be literate about the African diaspora.* Myers Education Press.

Boutte, G. S. and Strickland, J. (2008). Making African American culture and history central to teaching and learning of young children. *Journal of Negro Education, 77*(2), 131–142.

Boykin, A. W. (1994). Afrocultural expression and its implications for schooling. In E. Hollins, J. King, & W. Hayman (Eds.), *Teaching diverse populations: Formulating a knowledge base* (pp. 243–273). State University of New York Press.

Boykin, A. W., & Cunningham, R. T. (2001). The effects of movement expressiveness in story content and learning context on the cognitive performance of African American children. *Journal of Negro Education, 32*, 256–263.

Bronson, P., & Merryman, A. (2009). See baby discriminate. Kids as young as 6 months judge others based on skin color. What's a parent to do? *Newsweek, 154*(11), 52–60.

Bryan, N. (2018). Shaking "the bad boys": Troubling the criminalization of Black boys' childhood play, hegemonic White masculinity and femininity, and "the school playground-to-prison' pipeline." *Race, Ethnicity, and Education*.

Bryan, N. (2020). Remembering Tamir Rice and other boy victims: Imagining Black PlayCrit literacies inside and outside urban literacy education. *Urban Education*.

Bryan, N. (2021). *Toward a BlackboyCrit Pedagogy: Black boys, male teachers, and early childhood classroom practices*. Routledge.

Bryan, N., McMillan, R., & LaMar, K. (2022). Prison abolition literacies as pro-Black pedagogy in early childhood education. *Journal of Early Childhood Literacy, 22*(3), 383–407.

Delpit, L. (2012). What should teachers do? Ebonics and culturally responsive instruction. In *Dialects, Englishes, creoles, and education* (pp. 108–116). Routledge.

Derman-Sparks, L., & Ramsey, P. G. (2011). *What if all the kids are white?: Anti-bias multicultural education with young children and families*. Teachers College Press.

Dunham, Y., Baron, A. S., & Banaji, M. R. (2008). The development of implicit intergroup cognition. *Trends in Cognitive Sciences, 12*(7), 248–253.

Elliot, J. (31 July 2019). Charges tossed in the case of boy, 10, accused of dodgeball assault. Retrieved from https://globalnews.ca/news/5707201/boy-10-charged-assault-dodgeball/

Gaunt, K. (July, 2020). The magic of Black girls' play. Retrieved from https://www.nytimes.com/2020/07/21/parenting/black-girls-play.html

Gilliam, W. S., Maupin, A., Reyes, C. R., Accavitti, M., & Frederick, S. (2016), *Do early educators' implicit biases regarding sex and race relate to behavior expectations and recommendations of preschool expulsions and suspensions?* Yale Childhood Study Center.

Goff, P. A., Jackson, M. C., Di Leone, B. A. L., Culotta, C. M., & DiTomasso, N. A. (2014). The essence of innocence: Consequences of dehumanizing Black children. *Journal of Personality and Social Psychology, 106*(4), 526–545.

Gold, M. E., & Richards, H. (2012). To Label or Not to Label: The Special Education Question for African Americans. *Educational Foundations (26)*, 143–156.

Hale, J. E. (1982). *Black children: Their roots, culture, and learning styles*. Johns Hopkins University Press.

Hale-Benson, J. E. (1986). *Black children: Their roots, culture, and learning styles* (Rev. ed.). Johns Hopkins University Press.

Hale, J. E. (2001). *Learning while black: Creating educational excellence for African American children*. Johns Hopkins University Press.

Hart, B., & Risley, T. R. (1992). American parenting of language-learning children: Persisting differences in family-child interactions observed in natural home environments. *Developmental Psychology, 28*(6), 1096–1105.

Hilliard, A. G. (1992). Behavioral style, culture, and teaching, and learning. *Journal of Negro Education, 61*(3), 370–377.

Hirschfeld, L. A. (2008). Children's developing conceptions of race. In S. M. Quintana & C. McKown (Eds.), *Handbook of race, racism, and the developing child* (pp. 37–54). John Wiley & Sons, Inc.

Iruka, I., Curenton, S., Durden, T., & Escayg, K.(2020). *Don't look away: Embracing anti-bias classrooms*. Gryphon House.

Iruka, I., Durden, T., Escayg, K., & Curenton, S. (2023). *We are the change we seek: Advancing racial justice in early care and education*. Teachers College Press.

Jackson, J., Collins, S. N., Baines, J. R., Boutte, G. S., Johnson Jr, G. L., & Folsom-Wright, N. (2021). Back to Africa: lessons from the motherland. *The Social Studies, 112*(3), 120–135.

Katz, P. A., & Kofkin, J. A. (1997). Race, gender, and young children. In S. S. Luthar, J. A. Burack, D. Cicchetti, & J. R. Weisz (Eds.), *Developmental psychopathology: Perspectives on adjustment, risk, and disorder* (pp. 51–74). Cambridge University Press.

Kelly, D. J., Quinn, P. C., Slater, A. M., Lee, K., Gibson, A., Smith, M., & Pascalis, O. (2005). *Three-month-olds, but not newborns, prefer own-race faces*. Developmental Science, 8(6), F31–F36.

King, J. E. (2005). *Black education: A transformative research and action agenda for the 21st century*. Lawrence Erlbaum.

Kinloch, V. F. (2005). Revisiting the promise of students' right to their own language: Pedagogical strategies. *College Composition and Communication*, 83–113.

Kinzler, K. (2016, March 11). The superior social skills of bilinguals. *The New York Times*, SR10.

Ladson-Billings, G. (2009). *The Dreamkeepers: Successful teachers of African American children*. John Wiley & Sons.

Linguistic Society of America. (1997). *LSA resolution on the Oakland "Ebonics" issue*. Retrieved February 28, 2005 from https://www.linguisticsociety.org/resource/lsa-resolution-oakland-ebonics-issue

Love, B. L. (2016). Anti-Black state violence, classroom edition: The spirit murdering of Black children. *Journal of Curriculum and Pedagogy, 13*(1), 22–25.

Love, B. L. (2019). *We want to do more than survive: Abolitionist teaching and the pursuit of educational freedom*. Beacon Press.

Martin, J. (2017, October 13). *'You are my slave:' School's Civil War Day sparks mom's ire*. Associated Press. https://apnews.com/article/ f39d2500af6a44e48eab 4c3297999ca

Matias, C. E., & Allen, R. L. (2013). Loving whiteness to death: Sadomasochism, emotionality, and the possibility of humanizing love. *Berkeley Review of Education, 4*(2).

Milner IV, H. R., & Tenore, F. B. (2010). Classroom management in diverse classrooms. *Urban Education, 45*(5), 560–603.

Muhammad, G. (2020). *Cultivating genius: An equity framework for culturally and historically responsive literacy*. Scholastic.

Muller, M. (2021). Preparing Black children to identify and confront racism in books, media, and other texts: Critical questions. In *We be lovin' Black children: Learning to be literate about the African Diaspora*, Boutte, G., King, J., Johnson, G., & King, L. Myers Education Press, 37–45.

Okonofua, J. A., Walton, G. M., & Eberhardt, J. L. (2016). A vicious cycle: A social–psychological account of extreme racial disparities in school discipline. *Perspectives on Psychological Science, 11*(3), 381–398.

Owusu, P. (2019). Adinkra symbols as "multivocal" pedagogical/ socialization tool. *Contemporary Journal of African Studies, 6*(1):46–58.

Perry, T., & Delpit, L. (1998). *The real Ebonics debate: Power, language, and the education of African-American children*. Beacon Press.

Perry, T., Steele, C., & Hilliard, A. G. (2003). *Young, gifted, and Black: Promoting high achievement among African-American students*. Beacon Press.

Pinkney, A. D. (2010). *Sit-in: How four friends stood up by sitting down*. Little Brown Books for Young Readers.

Rickford, J. R. (1999). *African American vernacular English*. Blackwell.

Rickford, J. R., & Rickford, R. J. (2000). *Spoken soul*. John Wiley.

Rosen, R. (2017). Between play and the quotidian: inscriptions of monstrous characters on the racialised bodies of children. *Race, Ethnicity, and Education, 20*(2), 178–191.

Salaam, K. Y. (1978). *Revolutionary love: Poems and essays*. Ahidiana.

Sealey-Ruiz, Y. (2018). "The archaeology of the self", Future for Learning.

Shade, B. J. (1997). *Culture, style, and the educative process: Making schools work for racially diverse students* (2nd ed.). Charles T. Thomas.

Smitherman, G. (1977/1985). *Talkin and testifyin: The language of Black America*. Houghton Mifflin.

Smitherman, G. (2000). *Black talk: Words and phrases from the hood to the amen corner*. Houghton Mifflin Harcourt.

Smitherman, G. (2001). *Talkin that talk: Language, culture and education in African America*. Routledge.

Smitherman, G. (2006). *Word from the mother: Language and African Americans*. Routledge.

Souto-Manning, M. (2009). Acting out and talking back: Negotiating discourses in American early educational settings. *Early Child Development and Care, 179*(8), 1083–1094.

Souto-Manning, M. (2010). Challenging ethnocentric literacy practices:[Re] positioning home literacies in a head start classroom. *Research in the Teaching of English*, 150–178.

Souto-Manning, M., & Martell, J. (2017). Committing to culturally relevant literacy teaching as an everyday practice: It's critical!. *Language Arts, 94*(4), 252.

Sperry, D. E., Sperry, L. L., & Miller, P. J. (2019). Language does matter: But there is more to language than vocabulary and directed speech. *Child Development, 90*(3), 993–997.

Wheeler, R. S., Swords, R., & Carpenter, M. (2004). Codeswitching: Tools of language and culture transform the dialectally diverse classroom. *Language Arts, 81*(6), 470–480.

Wynter-Hoyte, K., Braden, E., Myers, M., Rodriguez, S. C., & Thornton, N. (2022). *Revolutionary love: Creating a culturally inclusive literacy classroom*. Scholastic.

Zaveri, M. (2020, February 27). Body camera footage shows arrest by Orlando police of 6-year-old at school. *The New York Times*. https://www.nytimes.com/2020/02/27/us/orlando-6-year-old-arrested.html

INDEX